Finding the World's Fullness

Books By Robert Cording

Poetry
Life-list (1987)
What Binds Us to This World (1991)
Heavy Grace (l996)
Against Consolation (2001)
Common Life (2006)
Walking with Ruskin (2010)
A Word in My Mouth: Selected Spiritual Poems (2013)
Only So Far (2015)
Without My Asking (2019)

Edited
In My Life: Encounters with the Beatles (1998)
(with Shelli Jankowski-Smith and E. J. Miller Laino)

Finding the World's Fullness

On Poetry, Metaphor, and Mystery

ROBERT CORDING

SL/.NT
BOOKS

FINDING THE WORLD'S FULLNESS
On Poetry, Metaphor, and Mystery

Slant Books
P.O. Box 60295
Seattle, WA 98160

www.slantbooks.com

HARDCOVER ISBN: 978-1-63982-025-2
PAPERBACK ISBN: 978-1-63982-024-5
EBOOK ISBN: 978-1-63982-026-9

Cataloguing-in-Publication data:

Names: Cording, Robert.

Title: Finding the world's fullness: on poetry, metaphor, and mystery. / Robert
   Cording.

Description: Seattle, WA: Slant Books, 2019

Identifiers: ISBN 978-1-63982-025-2 (hardcover) | ISBN 978-1-63982-024-5 (paper-
   back) | ISBN 978-1-63982-026-9 (ebook)

Subjects: LCSH: Religion and Poetry | Faith--Poetry | Metaphor in Literature | Spiri-
   tuality in Literature

Classification: PS3553.O6455 C5357 2019 (print) | PS3553.O6455(ebook)

Manufactured in the U.S.A.   10/05/21

*For the Reading Group—Bill, Bob, Jeff,
Jim, Joe, Mark; and always, Clyde and John*

... the field behind the hedge
Grew more distinctly strange as you kept standing
Focused and drawn in by what barred the way.

—Seamus Heaney, "Field of Vision"

We are sealed vessels afloat upon what it is convenient
to call reality; at some moments, without a reason,
without an effort, the sealing matter cracks; in floods reality. . . .

—Virginia Woolf, "A Sketch of the Past"

Contents

Preface

One of my earliest experiences with language was the sensation that words had physical properties—they could be heavy or light, serious or whimsical. And, even stranger, those properties seemed matched to the properties of the world around me. I have been writing poems now for some forty years. More than anything else, writing poems has kept me looking at the details of everyday experience, at what Richard Wilbur called the "hunks and colors of the world." Such looking has brought me face-to-face with the inescapable (and inscrutable) complexity of a world that is full of suffering and injustice, beauty and grace.

My project here has been to provide a rationale of sorts for what I broadly see as literature with a theological underpinning. My use of the word "theological" owes a debt to Czeslaw Milosz. In his book, *Second Space*, there is sequence of poems, called "A Theological Treatise." In the first poem, Milosz asks "Why theology? Because the first must be first. / And first is a notion of truth." Milosz certainly does not see himself as a possessor of Truth, as someone who is espousing this or that creedal belief. What he does believe in is the experience of the world itself: "When a thing is truly seen, seen intensely," Milosz writes, "it remains with us forever and astonishes us, even though it would appear there is nothing astonishing about it." Milosz wants to hold to something W. H. Auden once said about poetry: "there is only one thing / that all poetry must do; it must praise all it can for being / and for happening." As Milosz understands, Auden's statement expresses a theological belief.

My aim here has been to sketch a rationale for poetry that tries to take into account a world we did not make, being faithful to that essential mystery. Rooted in the belief that words can invoke what the critic George Steiner called "real presences," I look at how our attention to the concrete particulars of ordinary experience can bring us back, again and again, to the fundamental experience of being: that there is something rather than nothing.

I believe that there is a reality independent of our mental constructions. In the "Idea of Order at Key West," Stevens's woman must walk beside the sea to sing her song, even if the sea's own song is only meaningless plunges of water and wind. She may be the "single artificer of her song," but her song would not be possible at all without the sea. And, while I agree with Stevens that poetry's revelations are made possible by means of our language, I also want to hold to Richard Wilbur's acknowledgment that "The world's fullness is not made but found." I see poetry's task as one of helping readers find that fullness again and again.

one

The Readiness Is All

On Poetry and Mystery

Finding the "World's Fullness"

IWANT TO ARGUE WHY IT IS crucial to hold open the possibility that, as Richard Wilbur lovingly puts it, "the world's fullness is not made but found." Postmodern thought has called into question the dangerous illusions of self-possession and the dogmas surrounding our capacity to know. We have learned, certainly, to see the all-too-human interests that lie behind our words. Yet, if there is a pressing need at this time to deconstruct the old hierarchies, to remind ourselves of the mind's endless impositions of meaning, the process of doing so should still be to "discover an order as of / A season, to discover summer and know it . . . / Not to impose, not to have reasoned at all, / Out of nothing to come on major weather" (Wallace Stevens, "Notes Toward a Supreme Fiction"). The role of the arts and poetry in particular is always to bring us back to such primal moments. This task requires what Northrup Frye calls "double vision": the recognition of our own limits of understanding; and, after that, "perhaps the terrifying and welcome voice" that "annihilate[s] everything we thought we knew, and restore[s] everything we never lost."

In his late book, *Second Space*, there is sequence of poems which the Nobel Prize winner, Czeslaw Milosz, called "A Theological Treatise." In the first poem, Milosz says "a farewell to the decadence / Into which the language of poetry in my age has fallen" then asks "Why theology? Because the first must be first. / And first is a notion of truth." Milosz was never afraid to speak his mind. This poem lays out an intimate connection between theology and poetry.

We live in a time when the language of theological discourse, as Paul Mariani and others have pointed out, has been emptied of much of its former significance. In his essay, "Toward a Sacramental Language" in *God and the Imagination*, Mariani realizes that to live in a world that

3

denies the possibility of the sacred seems utterly and unnecessarily reductive. What we writers need, Mariani posits, especially those of us who do not accept the idea of "the totally alienated existentialist self," is "to shape a language that takes into account a world we did not make and that sees the necessity of making room for the sacred."

I want to use Milosz's clarion call of a poem to elaborate on three ideas: the decadence which Milosz feels the language of poetry has fallen into; the old and new relationship between theology and poetry as I see it; and the relationship between what Milosz later calls "reality" and "an absolute point of reference." My aim is to sketch what it means for our language "to take into account a world we did not make."

Let me begin with decadence. I cannot possibly provide a history of poetry. What I'll sketch here is, admittedly, no more than a sketch, replete with the half-truths of generalities. Some of what I'll say finds its source in Milosz's own essay, "Against Incomprehensible Poetry" from *To Begin Where I Am;* other parts are indebted to his Nobel Prize acceptance speech and to essays from a book entitled *Beyond Poststructuralism* edited by Wendell Harris.

For Milosz and many others, Western literature and art since the Renaissance have gradually become separated from Christianity. With humanism and the advent of the scientific worldview, the laws of instrumental reason were elevated at the expense of empathy and St. Paul's idea of faith seeking understanding. As Milton foresaw so well in *Paradise Lost,* humankind would soon become the center of its own world, the measure and maker, whose thinking could make a hell of heaven, and a heaven of hell. From Milton to Derrida, the confidence once enjoyed—that the metaphysical underwrites the physical world—has been called into question; for some today the world has no metaphysical dimension at all.

The critique goes something like this: the idea of an unmediated relationship between consciousness and an object, a relationship that is prior and uncontaminated by language, is a fiction because, as Derrida puts it, from "the moment there is meaning there are nothing but signs." If there are signs, then there is nothing like a pure relationship to presence.

The next step that many have taken, and that seems like a false step to me, is: if there is no pure presence, there is in effect no presence at all. There is only language, and we are lost in its labyrinths, in its fictions. And because we are enclosed in language, we are closed off from everything else. The poet in this little tale becomes the high priest of language. And poetry, to Milosz's dismay, becomes isolated, too esoteric for ordinary humanity and, perhaps worst of all, nothing but "experiments with form." "Western poetry," Milosz writes, "has recently gone so far down the path of subjectivity that it has stopped acknowledging the laws of the object. It even appears to be proposing that all that exists is perception, and there is no objective world." In short, the language of poetry has become incomprehensible and decadent.

The enemy for Milosz is always "speech entwining upon itself like the ivy when it does not find a support on a tree or wall" (Nobel Prize speech). Speech that entwines upon itself is speech that has "stopped acknowledging the laws of the object." What are these laws? What does Milosz mean by the "object"? For Milosz, and this will explain why I'm turning to him, the object can still be the site of epiphany. The object is not simply an entity that follows the laws of physics; neither is it something, which because we can only point at in words, cannot be known outside our own fictions of it. Rather, for Milosz, to acknowledge the laws of the object, to contemplate "tree or rock or a man," may bring us "to comprehend that it *is*, even though it might not have been."

In his essay, "Toward a Critical Re-Renewal," Quentin Kraft notes that we too often think there are only two opposing metaphors for our conception of language: for the poststructuralist crowd language is a "web, a labyrinth, a screen, a prisonhouse"; for, the traditionalists, language is a "glass, however dark and distorted, a window, a door and pathway." But there is a third way of thinking about language, Kraft argues, language as mediation. Here's the significant passage:

> . . . mediation is something that goes on in the middle; it is a medium, a means, something that intervenes between consciousness and an object. In that sense it separates. . . . But it also connects; it is what makes interaction possible; indeed it is an *interaction* and not a thing . . . more verb than noun, not anything statically situated between a person and the world, not a screen, but instead an activity or interaction going on in the space between. . . . In short, what is meant here by 'mediation' is presence, not the mythical pure presence but the actual adulterated presence, the only kind ever available to us.

Let me put my cards on the table: I believe that words point to and depend on a reality apart from the acts of verbal reference, though poetry and, to my mind, theology, is, as Stevens said, "a revelation in words by means of words."

That is, we live in a world that we did not create. This world of objects should force us out of ourselves, out of our subjectivity, since description, the task of the poet, demands attention, demands an attending to the world of objects. Description involves such intense observation, Milosz says in "Against Incomprehensible Poetry," that the "veil of everyday habit falls away and what we paid no attention, because it struck us as so ordinary, is revealed as miraculous." Or to say the same thing in the language of Wallace Stevens, poems should "refresh life"; they should help us see the world as if for the first time, free of what he called the "man-locked set" of our preconceptions.

For Milosz the decadence of poetry's language occurs when poets write out of the belief that words point only to other words, when we live inside what Milosz calls our own subjective "phantasmagoria." Though some might say the intense observation that Milosz calls for is just another form of self-indulgence or self-delusion, two counter arguments could be offered. First, as Milosz lays out in his Nobel Prize acceptance speech, the poet might be, in a perfect world, a "seeker of reality through contemplation." But, in fact, our world, and the world of Nazi Germany and Soviet Communism that Milosz grew up in, is deeply flawed, and such contemplation is negated by the demonic events of history. Thus the role of the poet for Milosz is one that must be lived in the "contradiction between art and the solidarity with one's fellow men," between contemplation of being and action. Milosz, like Simone Weil, whose philosophy meant so much to him, knows that the "contradictions the mind comes up against—these are the only realities: they are the criterion of the real." Secondly, and this follows on the point I've just made, Milosz is the first to admit (as he does in the third poem of his Treatise) that he is not, nor does he "want to be, a possessor of the truth." The truth he seeks does not find its end in the recitation of a creedal belief; rather it seeks the experience of the world itself. "When a thing is truly seen, seen intensely," Milosz writes, "it remains with us forever and astonishes us, even though it would appear there is nothing astonishing about it."

Thus Milosz wants to hold to something W. H. Auden said about poetry:

> Poetry can do a hundred and one things, delight, sadden, disturb, amuse, instruct—it may express every possible shade of emotion, and describe every conceivable kind of event, but there is only one thing that all poetry must do; it must praise all it can for being and for happening.

As Milosz understands, Auden's statement expresses a theological belief. Such affirmation of life has a long and distinguished past in Western thought, and it is precisely this affirmation that lies behind Milosz's question—"Why theology?" and his answer: "Because the first must be first." So we've come to the second point I want to elaborate: the relationship between poetry and theology.

Theology, of course, faces the same dilemma as poetry: its language, too, has been emptied of some of its former significance. And it, too, must take into account a world we did not make. I read a piece in *Tikkun* once by Marc Gafni titled, "On the Erotic and the Ethical," about the role of the Goddess, symbol of sacred eros, shared by both the temple and pagan cults in ancient Israel. Gafni writes, "The relationship with the Goddess was not a hobby for the Israelites like modern religious affiliation tends to be. It was an all-consuming desire to be on the inside, to feel the infinite fullness of reality in every moment and in every encounter. . . ." An "all-consuming desire to feel the infinite fullness of reality"—that is, I would say, what poetry and theology have always been trying to express. I've always felt that what lies behind the age-old impulse of literature to make itself new is just this sense of the erotic. When literature becomes mannered and parodic, as it has become during our own time, what we miss and yearn for is the "fullness of reality." To put it another way, the presence of the infinite fullness of reality is always waiting for us to be present. That is "the notion of truth" I think Milosz refers to in his poem and what he means when he instructs: "Let reality return to our speech." Since I don't want to pretend that I am a theologian, I want to illustrate the connection I see between poetry and theology by looking at what I do know—a poem by Wallace Stevens called "Not Ideas About the Thing But the Thing Itself." Here's the poem:

> At the earliest ending of winter,
> In March, a scrawny cry from outside
> Seemed like a sound in his mind.
>
> He knew that he heard it,
> A bird's cry, at daylight or before,
> In the early March wind.
>
> The sun was rising at six,
> No longer a battered panache above snow . . .
> It would have been outside.

It was not from the vast ventriloquism
Of sleep's faded papier-mache . . .
The sun was coming from outside.

That scrawny cry—It was
A chorister whose c preceded the choir.
It was part of the colossal sun,

Surrounded by its choral rings,
Still far away. It was like
A new knowledge of reality.

The situation is clear enough: the speaker hears a bird's cry in March and thinks of how the first bird heralds the returning flocks of birds; the bird is "a chorister whose c preceded the choir." As the title of the poem announces, the poem wants the thing itself and not ideas about the thing—on one level, the objective reality of the bird's cry beyond the mind. And yet, while we can know there is some "thing" outside our mind, as the speaker knows he heard the bird, as we move toward that thing in consciousness we lose it. (Since, to use Stevens's title, the mind's ideas of the thing compose their own world and we get ideas about the thing and not the thing itself). In the end, we can only know by analogy: "like / a new knowledge of reality."

Does that "like" in "Not Ideas" ("like / a new knowledge of reality") undercut the revelation? I don't believe it does. Working from the concept of language as mediation, it seems to me that the revelation—the knowledge of the bird's connection and our own to the choir and to the colossal sun that calls that choir and ourselves into being—remains intact precisely because of the simile. In my reading of Stevens's poem that last sentence is one of the most moving and authentic moments in poetry that I know.

In the last years of his life, after a lifetime of seeking for and trying to write the "poem of pure reality, untouched by trope or deviation," Stevens concludes "it was like / a new knowledge of reality." Through the poem, we encounter the impossible resurgence we call spring in all its colossal presence. And yet there is a second recognition as well: that what we encounter is also an experience of what remains hidden. That colossal presence is experienced from within the finitude and limitations of the human mind. And so it must be *like* a new knowledge of reality. I do not mean here to diminish the revelation in Stevens's last sentence. The speaker is compelled to announce that such a cry, such a colossal sun exists. He is compelled to recognize that our experience tells us there is a reality outside our mind's construction of it; and he is compelled to acknowledge that that reality, which lies outside the mind, can only be known inside the language the mind constructs for the reality. The truth of this poem and all poems that we value is not a proposition or judgment, not an insight that can be gained by simple transference, nor a message we can pass on to others, but rather an enactment of the bird's cry.

Stevens's poem, then, goes on in the "middle," it is "a medium, a means," to requote the Kraft essay, an interaction between consciousness and a bird early in March. Certainly it is true that Stevens, like many of the Modernist artists, saw the imagination as redemptive. Often, and wrongly I think, such statements have come to mean that the Modernists saw art as replacing religion, and saw the mind as the single "artificer," creating form and meaning out of meaninglessness. But the desire in late Stevens to "live in the world but outside of existing conceptions of it" is not a desire divorced from reality.

"Reality is a vacuum," Stevens declares in the *Adagia*, but in his essay titled "Imagination as Value," he writes, "The ultimate value is reality." The first statement seems to suggest that without the imagination we live in a world of dead objects, while the second suggests the primacy of the world. But when "reality is a vacuum" in Stevens, it is the reality we have become numb to, the world of objects that we so habitually see, we no longer notice. In a letter to Henry Church, Stevens wrote: "someone . . . wanted to know what I mean by a thinker of the first idea. If you take the varnish and dirt of generations off a picture, you see it in the first idea. If you think about the world without its varnish and dirt, you are a thinker of the first idea." The "ultimate value," then, *is* reality if we can see it "without its varnish and dirt."

What allows us to see reality "in the first idea" is metaphor. The "Supreme Fiction" that Stevens works towards but knows is impossible (thus his title "Notes Toward A Supreme Fiction") is, on the one hand, an acknowledgment that the poetic text is never complete because the metaphors poets employ to approach our intuitions of reality always break down. On the other hand we need a supreme fiction, not because it gives us the truth, but because it gives us a belief we can live by.

That belief, to return to Milosz, is that the world is, even though it might not have been. Such a belief is, indeed, an "absolute point of reference" because it says we did not create the world through our imagination. And yet the "ultimate value of reality" that we seek can only be known in language. The poet's obligation, then, is not to become a priest (as the Modernist dictum often had it) but rather to become priestly, to evoke the world in such a way that what "struck us as ordinary, is revealed as miraculous." The human search, then, is always for a language that can help us see the world again as if for the first time. What we listen for in the "sound of words," Stevens tells us is a "finality, a perfection, an unalterable vibration" ("The Noble Rider and the Sound of Words") that bring us closer (since metaphor always seeks to bring the world closer in its act of finding correspondences) to the "muddy center," the first idea, God.

Let me conclude by making some notes for the role of poetry. When Keats speaks of the "holiness of the heart's affections" and links those absolutes of imagination, beauty, and truth, he understands that poetry must have some ultimate purpose. So does Milosz. So did Wallace Stevens. So do I.

It is true, certainly, that we are alive in a historical moment in which the old truths are experienced as inadequate. But it is not a matter of the old truths being outdated or outstripped by our own age. Rather it is the living essence of our Hebraic and Hellenic roots that seems lost. As Northrop Frye has written, our tradition's founding religious language, our sense of its metaphorical integrity, becomes farther and farther removed from the experience that gave rise to its revelations and myths. As Stevens and Milosz well understand, it is necessary to break apart those acculturated values that stand between God and our conceptions of God. As Frye points out, "God may have lost his function as the subject or object of a predicate, but may not be so much dead as entombed in a dead language."

Wallace Stevens says we search for the "metaphor that murders metaphor." That is, we search for a language that murders our stale philosophical ideas, our outworn metaphors that keep us at a distance (that entomb God) rather than reenact the primordial moment of the transcendent. If we give up that search we also give up the world's fullness.

Cloud Shapes and Oak Trees

What...had been plain, dense cloud cover now took on land-scape-like formations, a chasm with long flat stretches, steep walls, and sudden pinnacles, in some places white and substantial like snow, in others gray and hard as rock....They hung over the town, muted red, dark-pink, surrounded by every conceivable nuance of gray. The setting was wild and beautiful. Actually everyone should be in the streets, I thought, cars should be stopping, doors should be opened and drivers and passengers emerging with heads raised and eyes sparkling with curiosity and a craving for beauty....However, a few glances at most were cast upward followed by isolated comments about how beautiful the evening was, for sights like this were not exceptional, on the contrary, hardly a day passed without the sky being filled with fantastic cloud formations...we lived our lives under the constantly changing sky without sparing it a glance or a thought. And why should we? If the various formations had some meaning, if, for example there had been concealed signs and messages for us, which it was important to decode correctly, unceasing attention to what was happening would have been inescapable and understandable. But this was not the case of course, the various cloud shapes and hues meant *nothing,* what they looked like at any given juncture was based on chance, so if there was anything the clouds suggested it was meaningless in its purest form.

—*My Struggle*, Karl Ove Knausgaard

As I was walking up to the church this morning I passed that row of big oaks by the war memorial . . . and I thought of another morning, fall a year or two ago, when they were dropping their acorns thick as hail almost. There was all sorts of thrashing in the leaves and there were acorns hitting the pavement so hard they'd fly past my head. All this in the dark, of course. I remember a slice of moon, no more than that. It was a very clear night, or morning, very still, and then there was such energy in all things transpiring among those trees, like a storm, like travail. I stood there a little out of range, and I thought, it is all still new to me. I have lived my life on the prairie and a line of oak trees can astonish me. I feel sometimes as if I were a child who opens its eyes on the world and sees things it will never know any names for and then has to close its eyes again.

—*Gilead,* Marilynne Robinson

NORWEGIAN CLOUDS AND Iowa oak trees. Both embody fantastic energy and mutability. Both are wild and beautiful. The shapes of the clouds and that hailstorm of acorns are the result of chance, or more accurately, in weather terms, the interchange of cold and warm fronts and the winds they produce. Knausgaard's clouds might be more excessive and beautiful than that line of oak trees in the town of Gilead. And, perhaps, as the narrator notes, they should awaken a "craving for beauty" in the drivers and passersby. But they do not. And, while it seems at first that the onlookers' indifference to the clouds' beauty might be their problem, the narrator goes on to explain that is not the case; the problem lies with what the passersby already know: the clouds do not conceal signs or messages. The varied cloud shapes and colors do not awaken anything in their viewers because they "meant nothing." And so, in the end, the clouds move into the soon-to-be-forgotten category of yet another pretty Norwegian sky.

Marilynne Robinson's oak trees astonish. They astonish despite the fact that, like the sky and clouds in Knausgaard, they are an ordinary sight, seen hundreds of times, even if not in this particular manifestation. What authorizes the "astonishment"? Many would answer that question as Knausgaard did: nothing at all. Marilynne Robinson, if you know her essays and books, might answer that question: the creation itself; the fact that we live in a created world and that faith, as she argues in a passage quoted by Anthony Domestico in *Commoweal*, is a "great, continuous instruction in perception itself," and to perceive correctly is to see "that the beauty that floods our senses has the meaning of vision and revelation."

Two different pictures of the same world, one that means "nothing" and one that has the meaning of "vision and revelation." Knausgaard's thinking is informed by a kind of natural thinking; the world is simply there, having moved from possibility to necessity. It's dense, opaque, beautiful, robust. But there is no point in looking for an origin for what is. Certainly Robinson doesn't think the falling acorns, the thrashing trees and that sliver of moon have meaning in and of themselves—are, that is, some kind of sign from God's book of nature which we can read. Even the "travail" that the narrator John Ames feels in the scene, has more to do with his psychological state than with what is actually taking place, which, as Robinson notes herself, is caused by the physical energies of the weather.

But Robinson's narrator brings another dimension to the scene: "I feel sometimes as if I were a child who opens its eyes on the world and sees things it will never know any names for." What does Ames open his eyes on? Well, oak trees. And yet those oak trees seem to be more than what Ames knows them as. Their name and even his knowledge of oak trees isn't adequate to the experience.

What is that experience? Perhaps it's best to let Robinson explain herself. In another passage she writes: when "a thing [in this instance, rainwater] exist[s] in excess of itself, so to speak, a sort of purity or lavishness, at any rate something ordinary in kind, but exceptional in degree." In that sense, it is not simply a matter of two scenes, one of clouds and one of oaks, and two different takes on the natural world, the first more secular, the second more religious. To talk that way, even if it is somewhat correct, would dismiss, at least in part, Robinson's notion of faith as quaint; I want to take her position seriously, both for her sake and my own, since I'll admit now, my own experience of the world is much like hers.

Robinson's shorthand for this kind of experience in *Gilead* is: "right perception is right worship." She is fully aware of the problems of using the word "perception." She knows its place in the Christian tradition, especially the Protestant tradition that places emphasis on one's individual experience, on having, as the Bible puts it, the eyes to see and the ears to hear. And she knows how the word has been denigrated in our daily usage; it often means no more than: "You see that cloud as a horse. I see a dog, and surely both our perceptions are equally valid."

Well, in that little scene they are. But Robinson has something wholly different in mind. Her usage of the the word "perception" involves both a specific understanding of the creation and the place of human beings and language in that creation.

Wallace Stevens, a poet Robinson loves, describes the kind of seeing Robinson has in mind in his poem "Angel Surrounded by Paysans":

> Yet I am the necessary angel of earth,
> Since, in my sight, you see the earth again,
> Cleared of its stiff and stubborn, man-locked set,
> And, in my hearing, you hear its tragic drone
> Rise liquidly in liquid lingerings.

Robinson, then, is talking about our experience of those moments when the ordinary and the extraordinary seem to tip into each other. Stevens's "angel of reality" posits a kind of primordial seeing, a seeing as if for the first time, the ordinary earth seen again, but cleared of "our stiff and stubborn, man-locked set" of preconceptions. Or as Stevens puts it in his poem, "The Latest Freed Man": "It was the importance of the trees outdoors, / The freshness of oak leaves, not so much / That they were oak leaves, as the way they looked. / It was everything being more real. . . ."

In his book, *The Experience of God,* David Bentley Hart describes the experience of this kind of perception: "it is the sudden awareness that no mere fact can possibly be an adequate explanation of the mystery in which one finds oneself immersed. . . ." For Hart, for me, and I think for Robinson, this mystery has to do with what Hart calls the "sheer inexplicable givenness of the world," the fact that anything at all exists.

In a *Paris Review* interview, Marilynne Robinson responds to the question, "Did you ever have a religious awakening?" with an emphatic "No, a mystical experience would be wasted on me." But what she goes on to say is pertinent here: "Ordinary things have always seemed luminous to me. One Calvinist notion deeply implanted in me is that there are two sides to every encounter with the world. You don't simply perceive something that is statically present, but in fact there is a visionary quality to all experience. It means something because it is addressed to you."

We might gloss the word "addressed" with "given." Marilynne Robinson's latest book of essays is aptly called *The Givenness of Things.* It is both an unfashionable book and an extraordinary book. At its core lies both the rehabilitation of the uniqueness of the human being, and the miraculous fact that we have a consciousness that makes the world intelligible to us. To quote Robinson, "The reality we experience is *given* (her italics) in the sense that it is, for our purposes, lawful, allowing hypothesis and prediction. . . ." There is, in short, a world already here; that this world need not be at all informs and shapes Robinson's thinking.

Let me sketch out this idea now more fully. My thinking here follows a line of thought that Robert Sokolowski lays out in his chapter, "Creation and Christian Understanding" in his book, *Christian Faith & Human Understanding*. Here is his starting point:

> The world, obviously, does exist. We start with that. But in Christian belief the world is understood as possibly not having been. The world becomes understood as existing in such a way that it might not have existed. And, in the Christian understanding if the world had not been, God would still be. . . . God is so understood that it would be meaningless to say that Creation added to his goodness, that he created out of any sort of need.

What follows from this premise are a different set of questions than, say, Aristotle would ask in inquiring into the being and substance of things. For Aristotle the problem would be: how did this animal or bird come to be this way; in the Christian understanding of creation, which is perfectly consistent with the "how" of evolution, the larger question is always: why does this animal or bird exist at all? And, if there is no reason for animal or bird to exist at all, and yet they do, God, who is self-subsistent, must have chosen to give them being.

To return to David Bentley Hart once more:

> One realizes that everything about the world is in fact charged with an immense and imponderable mystery. In that instant one is aware, even if the precise formulation eludes one, that everything one knows exists in an irreducibly gratuitous way: "what it is" has no logical connection with the reality "that it is."

As Sokowlowski puts it, "the fact that we are is the outcome of a personal transaction, not the outcome of chance or necessity, and it calls for a personal reaction on our part." It is just such a personal reaction that John Ames offers as he looks at the line of oak trees. For Marilynne Robinson, our thought and perception are the gifts that allow us to appreciate and be grateful for the gift of creation, of which those oak trees are a part. They can be "new" to John Ames over and over again because Ames's experience is one in which Hart's "that it is" overtakes, or isn't answered by "what it is." Or to re-quote Stevens, "It was everything being more real."

I want now to connect this experience of "everything being more real" to an essay by Martin Heidegger, "The Origin of the Work of Art." In this essay, Heidegger sets out to answer the question, "What is the mode of being of the work of art?" To ground this question, Heidegger looks, in part, at a Van Gogh painting of a pair of shoes. On the one hand, shoes, like tools and equipment in general, are made to be reliable, to function without their wearer having to give them a second thought. The more they function properly the less they are thought about. But in Van Gogh's painting we're made aware of a more complex reality. Wallace Stevens once defined reality as both a chair and all the life lived in it, and Heidegger wants us to see both the physical reality of the shoes and how Van Gogh's painting discloses the lived life of the peasant woman to whom these shoes belong. In the near-poem Heidegger makes of the painting, the shoes come alive: "In the stiffly rugged heaviness of the shoes there is the accumulated tenacity of her slow trudge through the far-spreading and ever-uniform furrows of the field swept by a raw wind. On the leather lie the dampness and richness of the soil. Under the soles slides the loneliness of the field-path as evening falls."

Van Gogh's shoes, and art in general, belong to the tension between what Heidegger calls "earth" (the reality of the non-human, "[the earth's] unexplained self-refusal in the fallow desolation of the wintry field"), and "the world" (the human context in which the peasant woman feels an "uncomplaining anxiety as to the certainty of bread, the wordless joy of having once more withstood want, the trembling before the impending childbed and shivering at the surrounding menace of death"). In this tension between earth and world (what Heidegger calls "strife"), Van Gogh's painting discloses what the shoes, both mere shoes and the life lived in the shoes, are "in truth," their "general essence." This double nature resides in the work of art itself, which is made of paint and yet transcends that material and allows the material to be more fully itself.

Heidegger's example here is a Greek temple. He points out that the marble we see in the temple is something quite different than the marble we saw in the quarry. The quarried marble now erected into a temple:

> draws out of the rock the mystery of that rock's clumsy yet spontaneous support. Standing there, the building holds its ground against the storm raging above it and so first makes the storm manifest in its violence. The luster and gleam of the stone, though itself apparently glowing by the grace of the sun, yet first brings to light the light of the day, the breadth of the sky, the darkness of the night. . . . The temple, in its

standing there, first gives to things their look and to men their outlook on themselves.

Heidegger goes on to draw a crucial distinction between equipment or things and a work of art: the work of art never uses up its material. Utilitarian objects exist simply in matter; they use up their material in the function of the material: bricks in a wall. But the work of art for Heidegger allows the material of its making to "shine forth," to be perceived in a way that they could not be perceived otherwise. In Van Gogh's painting the physical properties of the paint are formed into shoes, but, unlike the paint used to cover a wall, the painted shoes bring into the open the life lived in those shoes. They allow the shoes to be more fully perceived. In the strife between what wants to remain concealed and what wants to be revealed, the work of art (and I use "work" here, as Heidegger would have it, as a noun and a verb) allows the "happening of truth."

This truth is not Van Gogh's. And, while his talent as a painter is important, it is not his talent that allows the truth of the shoes to happen. "To create," as Heidegger says, "is to cause [or perhaps, a better translation here is "to let"] something to emerge as a thing that has been brought forth. The work's becoming a work is a way in which truth becomes and happens." The painting of the shoes allows the truth of the shoes to emerge the way the temple lets the shape of the sky and the darkness of the night emerge. That experience is one in which a pair of shoes exceeds itself as shoes, and, in the very excess of that exceeding, allows us to participate in the truth of what is opened before us. Participation is crucial to that verbal sense of "work" on which Heidegger insists. He calls this participation "preserving," and a work (noun) of art does not happen without the work (verb) of both creating and preserving.

In the "strife" of Van Gogh's painting, the shoes emerge as we participate in or interpret / preserve how field work can be both an intimate knowing of the earth and the impossibility of ever knowing the very earth which is worked; his peasant shoes hold each step across the fields in every season and at every time of day and night; and the shoes let the many emotions be felt which must have accompanied the woman who worked the fields or sat and watched the sun set, pooling in pinks and reds and purples across them; and it lets those moments emerge, perhaps, when the woman felt she knew some secret; and those so many other moments when the fields refused to yield anything more than what had been planted in the dirt.

I think writing like Marilynne Robinson's is rooted in the Heideggerian belief that it is in and through language that the world emerges in the fullness of its reality. Heidegger says, "Language alone brings what is, as something that is, into the Open for the first time." This phrase—"as something that is"—returns us to Wallace Stevens's "more real" oak trees and to Marilynne Robinson's oak trees that "astonish." The oak trees ("what is") seen in their Being ("as something that is") are seen in the perpetual newness of not needing to be at all. The revelation in words by means of words that Stevens speaks of returns us to the way language, and art in general, bring us back, again and again, to the fundamental experience of being: that there is something rather than nothing.

I often ask my students to write a statement regarding what they believe and what they would like their writing to accomplish. In short, why do they write? In that spirit, here's my own little credo. I believe words evoke and depend on a reality apart from the acts of verbal reference, though poetry and, to my mind, theology, is, as Wallace Stevens said, "a revelation in words by means of words."

I write, first and foremost, to honor the mystery of creation. Here are some of the assumptions that underlie my work: (1) this world is the only reality available to us; (2) it is a mystery; (3) in order to feel comfortable, we often end up loving what is imaginary—our own dreams and self-deceits; we reduce the mystery to our theories and explanations; (4) the "contradictions" the mind comes up against, as Simone Weil says, are the only realities (why, for example, the truly innocent suffer so much more than anyone could ever deserve); (5) those contradictions (as Weil has taught me) must be experienced to the very depths of our being—they are our cross; (6) what we suffer is our lived experience of the gap between the profound goodness of being and the painful, imperfect world human beings continue to create (as Wallace Stevens put it, we are an "unhappy people in a happy world"); (7) we must love this world—not to figure it out or even understand it, but as Wendell Berry says, "to suffer it and rejoice in it as it is"; (8) as a writer, I must try to shape a language that will take into account a world we did not make, being faithful to that essential mystery; at the same time, my language must try to faithfully record the terrifying and painful contradictions of human experience; and finally it must do so while remaining open to the intrinsic joy of being.

Of course, such statements of belief have all to do with those earlier conceptions of the cosmos that I sketched—if we conceive of being as random and meaningless, then there is no meaning to which our words can point. We can describe nothing but the play our words bring into existence. Within the Christian framework I'm speaking from, words are a gift, like the world itself and our existence. Words point to being that is intrinsically meaningful (the intuition of Genesis 1) rather than to a meaningless world on which meaning must be imposed. To say this does not mean I subscribe to a conception of language that is wholly transparent and non-distorting. Words conceal and reveal. Even in the most faithful verbal articulation something is added or subtracted, or both, from the experience we wish to write about.

Poetry never tries merely to mirror what science might call objective reality. As Stevens understood, and I referenced earlier, reality is not, say, a chair in a room that one might try to describe accurately. Reality is both the chair and the life lived in the chair: all those people who sat in it, read books, daydreamed, collapsed after a hard day's work.

Language seeks to evoke the lived sense of experience—the life lived in the chair. Metaphor, of course, never merely describes a fact; it seeks to evoke a sense of lived experience. When the psalmist says the "heavens declare the glory of God," he tries to evoke the literal stars; the sense that those stars "speak" because they cannot remain silent in the presence of God's glory, the utter wonder of what is and need not be. Truth, here, is not in the statement but in the experience to which the metaphor directs us.

Let me end by talking a little about the experience I want to evoke in my work. My task of late has been to evoke what I would call the primordial intuitions of Christianity. What are they?—that we live in a world we did not create; that God's immanent presence is capable of breaking in on us at every moment; that most of the time we cannot "taste and see" that presence because we live in a world of self-reflecting mirrors; that by attention alone—"that attention that is so full the 'I' disappears," as Simone Weil says, can we live in the world but outside of our existing conceptions of it.

This requires what Northrop Frye calls "double vision": the recognition of our own limits of understanding; and, after that, "perhaps the terrifying and welcome voice" that "annihilate[s] everything we thought we knew, and restore[s] everything we never lost." Eden is always with us. But it requires that we die to our human ways of knowing.

And so I write because in writing I sometimes unite my love and need. The work of writing helps me attend to a world I love but did not create. It is an act of soul-making that arises out of the need for the real work of our lives: the work we do not to acquire things but to be, to belong. I believe great poems allow us *to be* more vividly, if only for moments. Consider how the sound of a poem, the physical feel of its words, the sinews of its syntax, all seem to be brought suddenly into contact with its sense, and the poem's full resonance creates in us an elated sense of expansion. As the critic Sven Birkerts puts it, we "respond to the rightness of the verbal expression and, because of that rightness . . . suddenly grasp that the whole is welded together out of bits of sound. That organizations of sound mean—this is no less miraculous than the existence of physical laws. And both recognitions point in the direction of the first and last mystery that saturates the sacred writings of all cultures—that there is such a thing as being at all."

That a line of oak trees can astonish.

Acts of Attention
Some Thoughts on Poetry and Spirituality

Do you think of writing as a spiritual act at its core?

I do, because it involves a wonderful contradiction, which is
in order for it to happen you have to be there and you have to
disappear. Both. You know, nothing feels as good as that. . . .
Something happening through you, but you're attending it. There
are few other things in the world like that, but writing is pretty
much a relief from the self—and yet the self has to be utterly
there.

—From an interview with Marie Howe, at The Millions

IN HIS POEM "TWO TRAMPS in Mud Time," Robert Frost's speaker
looks for a reason why, when two out-of-work lumberjacks approach
him as he splits wood on a beautiful April day, he doesn't give them the
job. Part of him can freely acknowledge that he "ha[s] no right to play
/ With what [is] another man's work for gain." But another part of him
has already been given over to the work itself, to the delight of swinging
an axe on an early spring day in New England. Here's Frost:

> The time when most I loved my task
> These two must make me love it more
> By coming with what they came to ask.
> You'd think I never had felt before
> The weight of the ax-head poised aloft,
> The grip on earth of outspread feet,
> The life of muscles rocking soft

And smooth and moist in vernal heat.

The day has already given "loose to [his] soul," freeing him to feel the bounty of a first New England spring day when the "the sun [is] warm, but the "wind [is] chill" and every wheel-rut is a brook, gurgling with spring run-off. Lost in his work, in his own body, in the good weather, Frost is fully absorbed by the enjoyment of his activity. Consider those lush, rocking iambs as Frost lingers over the pleasure of "the life of muscles rocking soft / and smooth and moist in vernal heat." Thus, if he gives his work to the unemployed tramps, he will lose more than a few bucks. Yet, when the speaker finally gives his reason why he will send the unemployed tramps away and continue to split his own wood, he turns to a nobler explanation:

> My object in living is to unite
> My avocation and my vocation
> As my two eyes make one in sight.
> Only where love and need are one,
> And the work is play for mortal stakes,
> Is the deed ever really done
> For Heaven and the future's sakes.

This nobler explanation is part truth, part rationalization. On the one hand, Frost wants us to see why he cannot part with his own enjoyment, even when others need the work for food. On the other hand, he wants us to acknowledge that the aim of living is indeed the union of our avocation and vocation. To put the matter a little differently, Frost's poem creates the experience of those moments when we step outside linear time, when the rhythms of work connect with the rhythms of nature, and we live inside one of the inmost truths of religion—that there is an integral rightness to life. In that sense, our work is indeed for "mortal stakes," because in those activities where we unite our avocation and vocation, we return once again to the lost Eden where work once expressed the creative will of creation. Work, that is, resumes its deep connection to "play," when our labor is not toil (even if it is hard) because all our energies are concentrated in the activity itself, and the "I" that too often sees itself toiling, disappears.

As Aristotle knew, for our lives to be complete, there must be something that we desire to do for its own sake—something that is not a means to an end, but an end in itself. The "revelation" in Frost's poem occurs when Frost suddenly feels the grip of his feet on the earth, the weight of the axe-head poised in the air, the fluid movement of his muscles, and the intimate connection between his work and the preciousness and precariousness of an April day in New England. Frost understands with his whole body the truth which is evident: that our labor can return, if only temporarily, the ease and unselfconsciousness we had before the Fall when "love and need" were one. Here's that "wonderful contradiction" Marie Howe speaks of, for the speaker is both "utterly there" and "not there," fully aware of the day, the sky and clouds, the bluebird nearby, the feel of his axe swinging and the sound of the oak splitting on the chopping block, but he has disappeared. In Howe's words, "Something is happening through you, but you're attending it."

We all know too well how life often goes by without our seeing it. In Wallace Stevens's poem, "Man on the Dump," the speaker acknowledges, "the dump is full of images"—full, that is, of the stale ways we look at the world until we no longer see it. What Stevens's speaker wants is a "purifying change," a way of seeing "as a man" and "not like an image of a man." The poem ends in a barrage of questions, the man on the dump (in part, Stevens the poet, trying to cast off his poetic precursors in whose images he keeps seeing the world) casting aside those old images of truth, and hoping to see the world freshly, to come near to that moment when we first heard of the truth: "The the." Elsewhere, Stevens calls this moment "the first idea." In a letter to Henry Church, he describes this first idea metaphorically, asking Church to imagine a painting that has been covered with the grime of years. That dirt and grime, Stevens explains, are all the filters through which we see the world. But if the painting were to undergo a cleaning, we would see it afresh, as if for the first time.

Stevens is the first to admit just how difficult such seeing is. But he knows, like Emerson and Thoreau before him, that we cannot understand the world by distancing ourselves from it or framing it in objective terms. To behold the world, we need, Stevens knows, to return to something we may have forgotten, or at best distorted: wonder. In their book, *Practicing Mortality*, Christopher Dustin and Joanna Ziegler point out that "wonder is not just a subjective response to things. It is not just something we do. For the Greeks, things are (or are not) 'wonders.' We may be able to see this, or we may fail to see it, but the 'wonder' is something that stands before."

The older we get, the farther away we seem from those deep responses to the world we once had as children. It is no accident that in Tolstoy's great story, "The Death of Ivan Ilyich," Ivan, opening himself at last to the possibility that he has not truly lived, begins to think of childhood as the one authentic time of his life. For him, and for most of us, living according to "propriety," or living without truly realizing what life is, brings on the gathering weight of death. What Ivan Ilyich does not want to admit, even to himself, is that all his choices were dictated not by what he loved, but rather by what society prized. His experience of life has been second hand, routine.

So what does it mean to attend to this world and, at the same time, for the self that is doing the attending, to disappear? When I say attend, I do not simply mean the physiological act of seeing with one's eyes. If I hear Marie Howe and Robert Frost correctly, there is in such seeing a perception of the fullness that exists in each moment. The philosopher Martin Heidegger would say such seeing means following "the path of a responding that examines as it listens." Responding and examining: in other words seeing always involves more than accurate scientific observation, though such observation is crucial. But seeing is impossible without love or reverence. That is, seeing is an exercise in overcoming one's self, in attending to something quite particular other than oneself. Only the detachment of love helps us to see what there is to see as opposed to what we expect to see or are determined to find.

But why is it so hard to see? Why does a word like "behold" seem so nostalgic? I think there's a convincing analysis of our contemporary situation in Heidegger's 1955 essay, "The Question Concerning Technology." Heidegger's central insight is that technology is not simply a means to an end, which, like any tool, is at our disposal. To him, that kind of thinking makes us "blind to the essence of technology" and to the fact that we "remain unfree and chained to technology whether we affirm or deny it." The essay traces the reasons for this enchainment. First, Heidegger looks at the Greek conception of techne or craft, from which technology arises. He argues that we have lost the ancient Greek connection to what techne originally meant. For Heidegger, techne, is a "bringing forth" as opposed to a "bringing about." That is, the craftsman does not cause something to happen so much as occasion its happening. Craft, then, is not simply the imposition of form on matter; it also allows form and matter to appear.

Think of the way an architect uses stones, but does more than put them to use, allowing the material qualities of the stone, its patterns and textures, to appear. Or the way a gardener prepares the soil, sows the seeds, waters, and weeds so the plants will flourish, but understands that the germination of the seeds, their flowering and fruition, are not in the gardener's hands.

The problem, then, is that this original relationship to techne has been lost. Modern technology is no longer a matter of "bringing forth" but rather of what Heidegger calls "challenging" or "setting upon." In the modern technological view, the world we live in is no longer a source, something we work with to bring forth its inherent possibilities, but a resource at our disposal. While modern technology provides a greater supply of basic necessities (we can eat fruits and vegetables out of season, "stockpile" electricity to use when we want it, turn summer into winter with air conditioning), it also occludes our relationship to the world. Technology enchains us, in Heidegger's view, because it takes away our sense that we still owe our lives to something we did not make.

When the world is at our disposal, Heidegger argues, it no longer matters in the same sense as it once did. It can only reveal itself as something to be utilized rather than as a source to which we owe a debt. Modern technology keeps us from seeing how everything is not within our control. The result for Heidegger is that: "the impression comes to prevail that everything man encounters exists only insofar as it is his construct. This illusion gives rise in turn to one final delusion: It seems as though everywhere and always man encounters only himself."

To encounter ourselves everywhere we go is, of course, to lose all sense of wonder. Perhaps wonder begins with paying attention to our experience of being alive. Consider the dizzying number of passages that read like notations in Thoreau's *Walden* or his journals. Speaking of the ice leaving Walden Pond, Thoreau writes "In 1845, Walden was open on the 1st of April; in '46, the 25th of March; in '47, the 8th of April; in '51, the 28th of March; in '52, the 18th of April, in '53, the 23rd of March; in '54, about the 7th of April." Writing of early May birds, Thoreau notes, "I saw a loon in the pond, and during the first week of the month, I heard the whippoorwill, the brown thrasher, the veery, the wood-pewee. . . ." There are descriptions of the behavior of box turtles, seasonal temperature changes, the color variations in leaves, the croaks of bullfrogs.

I think the underlying assumption in all of these notations is that we owe the world our attention. Thoreau pays attention to each particular phenomenon. He is always dropping a thermometer into Walden Pond or taking its measurements, or, lying on his stomach, looking at ice bubbles. He was as good and passionate an observer as they come. His boast that, reawakened after death, he could tell you what day of the year it was, give or take a few days, is probably worth betting on.

Likewise, in *Modern Painters*, Ruskin devoted whole sections to Rocks, Water, and Clouds, and he recommended to his students that they follow his lead and each morning, as a daily exercise, draw the clouds they found in the dawn sky. His cloud studies are meticulous renderings; Ruskin often notes the place, as well as the time and wind's direction. Once, at the Ashmolean museum in Oxford, I spent hours looking at his drawings; I was lost in and delighted by the scientific attention Ruskin gave to the most ordinary objects—weathered boards on the Old Bridge at Lucerne, strawberry leaves, an oak branch in winter, a closed and open rose, a feather from a kingfisher. Of course, there were the more famous architectural drawings of his trips to the Alps and Italy, but it was clear that Ruskin gave the same attention to a leaf as he did to a mountain range or a church. He attended to the particulars that make each thing distinct.

When I first started to write poems in college and graduate school, I wanted to write about the natural world, which has always been an important part of my life. But I realized that, despite knowing a few flowers and trees, I really didn't know much at all. I made a plan. I'd fill a backpack with field guides, walk into the woods, and move forward only when I could name everything around me. I never got very far.

But I learned a few things. First, that just as when I taught, I needed to learn the names of the students in my class to establish, at the very least, their uniqueness, I also needed, as a kind of courtesy to the uniqueness of the flora and fauna just outside my door, to know the names of trees and birds and flowers. Second, I learned that knowing the name of a bird or a tree was just that: knowing a name. As with my students, there was so much more. I learned quickly how much more study it would take to understand the bird's behavior, its mating patterns, its various songs, what Hopkins called its "thisness." And third, I found myself thinking about how often my idea of what was real differed from what was actually there. Flowers that I thought I knew turned out to have more petals than I'd assumed, or the leaves were arranged alternately rather than symmetrically.

Even when I thought I knew something well, it often turned out I had barely scratched the surface. Once, a biologist at the college where I taught who'd heard I was a bird-watcher, asked me if I knew what bird sounded like zip, zip, zip, tseee. I quickly answered, "a warbler," like some star pupil. She could barely hold back her laughter. Ever so politely, in that knife-like, understated, academic manner, she asked, "yes, but *what* warbler?" I learned how hard it was to see and hear; I learned, too, that the seeing and hearing, which I thought were a given (I had eyes and ears that worked), actually required discipline and practice. And something more.

While I knew from my interest in religion about the *via negativa*, the practice of "cleaning house" or negating all humanly constructed images of God in order to allow in the immanent energies of God, I began to see how "seeing" required the same kind of house cleaning. Thoreau once said, "I begin to see an object when I cease to understand it." Thoreau refers here to the illusory power that knowledge can confer. When we think we understand something, our thinking often ends. But the world we live in is multi-layered, dense, and has an amplitude which we can sense, but never fully know. We cannot sum up the experience of being alive with a list of what we did from hour to hour. It's a disquieting feeling mostly: that there is another dimension to life which we feel, and perhaps even see and live at moments, but which, for the most part, remains in the background.

My contention here is that attention has something to do with a practiced look at this background. Again, I don't mean to suggest that some curtain or veil is pulled back and the great ta-da of God is revealed; in fact, I mean quite the opposite—that attention is simply a loving look at what is. I think we come to know the world not by detaching ourselves from our felt experience, but by inhabiting our bodily experience as richly and wakefully as we can—what Gerard Manley Hopkins described as our experience of the "dearest freshness deep down things." An act of attention, then, helps us to actualize our capacity to see this "dearest freshness." As the Polish poet and Nobel Laureate, Czeslaw Milosz writes, "When a thing is truly seen, seen intensely, it remains with us forever and astonishes us, even though it would appear there is nothing astonishing about it." For Milosz, to contemplate "tree or rock or a man" may bring us "to comprehend that it is, even though it might not have been." In a late prose poem called "The Watering Can," Milosz, writes that

> "in our clinging to distinctly delineated shapes, does our hope
> reside, of salvation from the turbulent waters of nothingness
> and chaos."

I began with a poem about swinging an axe; here's one about a pitchfork. It's by Seamus Heaney, a poet who attends as well as any writer I know. I want to consider both how well Heaney delineates the shape and feel of the pitchfork, and how he moves, as all poems must, from description to metaphor. The poem is from his wonderfully titled book, *Seeing Things*. It opens with a two-line statement, joining two unlikely words: "implement" and "perfection": "Of all implements, the pitchfork was the one / That came near to an imagined perfection." The writer's task is set: how is the common pitchfork, an implement right for pitching hay, also one that stirs the speaker to imagine perfection? The poem then turns to delineating the pitchfork:

> When he tightened his raised hand and aimed with it,
> It felt like a javelin, accurate and light.
>
> So whether he played the warrior or the athlete
> Or worked in earnest in the chaff and sweat,
> He loved its grain of tapering, dark-flecked ash
> Grown satiny from its own natural polish.
>
> Riveted steel, turned timber, burnish, grain,
> Smoothness, straightness, roundness, length and sheen.
> Sweat-cured, sharpened, balanced, tested, fitted.
> The springiness, the clip and dart of it.

The pitchfork as a Platonic perfect form. How does Heaney get away with such a claim?—by attending to the pitchfork, by letting the pitchfork be in all the particulars of its ash-flecked grain, its naturally patinaed-sweat-cured-lathe-turned shaft; by letting the reader feel the light heft of it, the springy strength of its tines, and how, holding it, one feels both its purpose—the lifting and tossing of hay—and how it would fly from the hand, like a javelin, if thrown. This is an implement that joins work and play. It lets the imagination fly:

> And then when he thought of probes that reached the farthest,
> He would see the shaft of a pitchfork sailing past
> Evenly, imperturbably through space,
> Its prongs starlit and absolutely soundless—
>
> But has learned at last to follow that simple lead
> Past its own aim, out to an other side
> Where perfection—or nearness to it—is imagined
> Not in the aiming but the opening hand.

Those springy tines have become space probes, the pitchfork now hurling soundlessly through space. The simple act of attending to the pitchfork and its javelin-like flight has led Heaney beyond himself, towards an "other side" where perfection might be imagined, but cannot be had, especially by "aiming" to have it. We can only attend and let go; we can only be here with the pitchfork and, with imagination, "there" where it flies to, beyond the self.

I think the best art always involves such loving attention to what is before us. I would argue that art is not about the will; that making art should push aside the ego and desires of the artist; and that this pushing aside can only take place in the absorption of the artist by what is actual. Maintaining the integrity of the work itself is the artist's form of love since, as soon as the artist tries to please, the good of the thing that is being made will be compromised.

Great art, then, isn't a statement of truth, nor is it aimed at the good of humanity because it does not try to tell us anything; rather, if the artist fixes his or her attention on something real, what is made will be beautiful "because it will be transparent to what is always present in the real, that is the overflow of presence which generates joy." This last statement is from a wonderful book-length meditation called *Grace and Necessity* by the former Archbishop of Canterbury, Rowan Williams, that informs much of what I have just said here.

Williams's book is a reflection on the aesthetic theory of the Catholic philosopher, Jacques Maritain. What I love about this little book is the way it revolves around two phrases of Maritain's about "things being more than they are" or "not only what they are." I want to end by briefly exploring these phrases. The artist in Williams's book "perceives the material of the world—visible things, patterns of sound, texture, as *offering more than can appear in one moment of encounter.*" Think of how artists have tried to solve that dilemma—Monet's many views of the same haystacks in different light and seasons; or the multiple perspectives of Faulkner's *The Sound and the Fury*; or the montage of voices in Eliot's *The Waste Land*. Everyone who has ever painted or written a word wants his or her work to embrace everything at once—Wal-Mart and a bluebird, grocery shopping and ecstasy. And everyone fails.

But, while that kind of failure is inevitable, what matters for Williams and Maritain is the degree to which an artist is attentive or obedient to what is being encountered. To Rowan Williams that attention is made manifest in a work of art by the degree to which, as Williams says, it has "dimension" outside of its relation to the artist. He writes, "There is the sense that the world 'gives' itself to be understood in the very moment when we realize that describing it simply in terms of how it relates to me, let alone serves my interest, is an inadequate or actively untruthful perspective."

For me, this line of thought brings back a passage from *Gilead*, in which John Ames, the minister/narrator remarks, "This is an interesting planet. It deserves all the attention you can give it." Though he is no philosopher, his homespun language may catch what I've been after best of all. Recalling a young couple on a stroll after rain, he thinks about the way the sun "just shone" and the tree "just glistened" and the water "just poured" that day, calling attention to the word "just." He concludes that people use the word "just" in that manner when they "want to call attention to a thing existing in excess of itself."

For me, attention in general, and the artist's loving attention more specifically, is always a commitment to that excess, that sense of how the world we live in exceeds mere functionality or need. In such moments, we attend entirely to something else, disappearing in the process.

Love Calls Us to One World at a Time

A FEW DAYS BEFORE HIS death on May 6, 1862, Henry David Thoreau was asked by Parker Pillsbury, a former minister become abolitionist, that question so many would like to have answered. Noting that Thoreau was "near the brink of the dark river," Pillsbury asked Thoreau how the "opposite shore" appeared to him. Thoreau, according to the biographer Richard D. Richardson, "summed up his life" with his answer: "One world at a time."

Thoreau's reply, polite but firm, was in accord with the way he deliberately chose to live his life. Just months before his death, he was still collecting material for projects on the succession of forest trees and seed dispersal, newly taken with nature's economy of abundance and its genius of vitality. Years earlier, in *A Week on the Concord and Merrimack Rivers,* Thoreau had come to a similar understanding: we need, he said, "not only to be spiritualized, but naturalized, on the soil of the earth. . . . We need to be earth-born as well as heaven-born."

Thoreau, who is too often mistakenly placed under the convenient label of pantheist, was not choosing to be "earth-born" over and against being "heaven-born." He believed, rather, that both births depended on each other. To be "heaven-born" did not lie in redirecting attention from the natural to the supernatural, but in seeing more deeply into the sources of the natural. Those sources, like creation itself, were always a mystery.

In his famous poem, "Love Calls Us to the Things of This World," Richard Wilbur enacts the way love calls us to extend ourselves towards a world which will always remain irreducible in its otherness and yet open to our understanding and recognition. In Wilbur's poem, the soul cannot exist free of the body's restrictions. Each day it must learn to keep a "difficult balance" in a world which asks us, as Wendell Berry has said, "to suffer it and rejoice in it as it is."

As Thoreau's life had taught him, if we try to leave behind the earth, if we choose religion simply to quiet our fears and prop up our hopes rather than connect us with the sources of life, we ignore the call of love and heed only the usual summons of the self and its needs.

I want to explore, then, the "difficult balance" of being both earth- and heaven-born and how such birth requires that we "crave reality" as Thoreau put it in *Walden*. I want also to connect Thoreau's adamant "one world at a time" to the way poetry, and art in general, can be, as Iris Murdoch has argued in her book *Metaphysics as a Guide to Morals*, both "contingent limited historically stained stuff" and, nevertheless, a "source of revelation" that helps us experience those intimations of a world that is fuller and more real, and is and is not the very world we or- dinarily move about in unawares. And I want to connect both these ideas to love—that loving the world and creating a work of art both require what Murdoch calls "morally disciplined attention" to "something quite particular other than oneself."

As my friend and colleague at Holy Cross, Chris Dustin, has said in an essay on Thoreau's religion, "Thoreau's vision of nature points be- yond nature, to a divinely creative source. As such, it incorporates a form of religious transcendence that is seldom recognized. As Thoreau sees it, nature points beyond itself, to a transcendent ground that is neither separable from it nor reducible to it." Dustin goes on, "Thoreau's point is not that we should forsake our heavenly aspirations, but that heavenly aspirations not bound to earth are not heavenly enough." To be "earth- born" involves a "drawing near," as Thoreau put it, to the world around us, and to draw near demands our exacting attention.

Thoreau was as good a practicing naturalist as they come. He measured, he took careful notes; he made comparisons, even ran experi- ments. But Thoreau was a scientist who recognized that seeing also re- quires more than objectivity and close scrutiny. Rather than understand the world by distancing himself from it, or by framing it in objective terms, Thoreau wanted to "commune" with nature because he was look- ing for a way to participate in a fullness which both overflowed and yet was rooted in actual things. Yet he never presumed to understand na- ture's "great secret" because his experience of nature taught him that any understanding would be a reduction, a limiting of nature to the terms of his understanding.

Thoreau's faith was in the world around him. That faith did not involve a state of mind or a creed so much as a movement toward mak- ing the "real world as real as possible," as Gary Snyder has put it. It was a faith that was rooted in that moment when we "return to our senses." Here's Thoreau in his essay "Walking":

> I am alarmed when it happens that I have walked a mile into the woods bodily, without getting there in spirit. . . . It sometimes happens that I cannot easily shake off the village. The thought of some work will run in my head and I am not where my body is—I am out of my senses. In my walks I would fain return to my senses.

We might say that our usual, daily experience of the world we live in is quite close to what Thoreau is getting at in his phrase "out of my senses." We eat reading the morning paper, rush off to work in cars or public transportation passing by those things we have seen each day for years and have long lost sight of, and finally reach work, our minds rehearsing what must be done and inventing that daily to-do list that never, of course, gets entirely done.

But we also know those moments when we "return to our senses," when the world suddenly stands forth, and we "behold," as Wallace Stevens has said, "a kind of total grandeur . . . with every visible thing enlarged and yet / no more than a bed, a chair. . . ." I mean here our capacity to perceive the fullness which exists in each moment and is always waiting for us to be present to it—what the novelist Marilynne Robinson referred to in *Gilead* as a "thing existing in excess of itself."

Each of us has had countless experiences of being "returned to our senses"—when, say, the field we are walking through, or the city street we are walking down, suddenly captivates us, and the trees in the distance and the way they align with the field's grasses and contours, or the buildings and the play of light on them and the people walking, all feel as if they belong exactly as they are.

And we, too, are part of that belongingness; and the field, the trees, the light, the buildings are all part of a deeper, more real, reality. This experience is both ordinary and extraordinary, and involves mystery (from the Greek *mysterion*). I'm using mystery here not to refer to the unknown but rather to the quality of the known; to refer to awe rather than ignorance. We can never be finished with mystery—like beauty, it is not governed by concepts and it does not allow a conclusion. It goes beyond all the evidence. In his book, *The Demon and the Angel*, the poet Ed Hirsch quotes a line from Lorca found at the bottom of a drawing Lorca did in Buenos Aires: "Only mystery enables us to live."

Yet, as moderns we are all too ready to say belief in mystery is nostalgic. Caught in our positivist moment, we limit the meaning of mystery to that which is unknown. We then point to the inevitable acquisition of further knowledge which will reduce that which is unknown and, eventually, erase the unknown entirely.

In a speech given at the World Economic Forum in 1992, Vaclav Havel, the Czech dissident who later became the President of Czechoslovakia, argued that the modern era has been dominated by the mistaken belief that the "world—and Being as such—is a wholly knowable system governed by a finite number of universal laws that man can grasp and rationally direct for his own benefit." Speaking to the need for a new kind of political order, Havel saw the abandonment of "the arrogant belief that the world is merely a puzzle to be solved" as a first step. Instead of our ill-conceived belief in universal systemic solutions, Havel called for trust "not only [in] a scientific representation and analysis of the world, but also the world itself . . . not only in sociological statistics, but also in real people . . . not only [in] an objective interpretation of reality, but also his own soul . . . his own thoughts . . . his own feeling."

Now Havel may sound too much like he's trumpeting a return to Romanticism. I don't think so. His repetition of the phrase "not only" is crucial here. Havel knows full well that the self-centeredness and other-worldliness of Romanticism simplified our view of the inner life and led, ironically, to the pendulum-swing towards a narrow objectivity. But he knows, too, that our belief that we know everything we need to know for the purposes of life is not only arrogant but deforming.

As Iris Murdoch has pointed out in *Existentialists and Mystics*, our "simple-minded faith in science, together with the assumption we are all rational and totally free, engenders a dangerous lack of curiosity about the real world, a failure to appreciate the difficulties of knowing it." I have turned to Thoreau's notion of "earth-born" because I feel that he, like Simone Weil in the twentieth century, provides a much needed vocabulary of attention, where attention is the opposite of willfulness, and demands a continual and careful devotion to a reality which as Murdoch says, "we are constantly and overwhelmingly tempted to deform by fantasy."

Thoreau's attentiveness is a kind of spiritual discipline, an exercise of constantly attending to the uniqueness and particularity of the world around him. In doing so, Thoreau helps us think about what Murdoch calls "the transcendence of reality," those moments I have tried to describe when we are returned to our senses and experience the joy which Weil defined as the "overflowing consciousness of reality." It is a moment of transfiguration where the ordinary becomes extraordinary without becoming otherworldly. Thoreau also makes us realize that when we rush to be "heaven-born" we lose sight of the particulars of the world, and often end up worshiping our ideas about life rather than life itself. We need to heed Czeslaw Milosz's warning: "Little animals from cartoons, talking rabbits, doggies, squirrels, as well as ladybugs, bees, grasshoppers. They have as much in common with real animals as our notions of the world have with the real world. Think of this and tremble" ("A Warning").

Part of Milosz's greatness as a writer lies in his willingness to "tremble." Milosz fought against the late-twentieth-century tendency to adore "the labyrinth of his mind" ("Labyrinth"), knowing that, while no one expected an answer from "questions addressed to the sky, the earth, to stars and clouds" in our time, there was still the "that, ready, formed in every detail" and "already existing" ("That"). Like Wallace Stevens's attempts to describe "The the," there is always in Milosz a world already existing that Milosz seeks to discover. Yet, even after ninety years of describing "countries, cities, gardens, the bays of the sea," Milosz knows that they are always waiting to be "described better than they were before" ("Late Ripeness").

Here is Milosz in the first essay of his selected essays; it is called "My Intention": "I am always aware that what I want is impossible to achieve. I would need the ability to communicate my full amazement at 'being here' in one unattainable sentence." As a result, Milosz's writing is a process of self-correction—on the one hand, he recognizes the incurable illness of our self-delusions; on the other, he sees that his task as a poet is to restore the "lost face of the world" (see "A Semi-Private Letter About Poetry").

My interest in Milosz is twofold: he is a writer who is at once quintessentially modern, aware that "human speech cannot encompass any phenomenon in its total roundness" ("Letter to Jerzy Andrzejewski") and that human beings can be cartoonish in the way they ape social fashions and ideas; and he is resolutely old-fashioned in his belief that human nature is fundamentally attracted to the goodness of creation. His poems suffer in the in-between of these two poles: "On one side there is luminosity, trust, faith, the beauty of the earth; on the other side, darkness, doubt, unbelief, the cruelty of the earth, the capacity of people to do evil" ("A Goal"). Milosz, like Martin Buber, like the Thoreau I have tried to capture, emphasizes what Buber called the "lived concrete"; that is, "the meaning of existence is open and accessible in the actual lived concrete, not above the struggle with reality, but in it."

Implicit in what I have been saying is the role of the artist and art. Milosz's willingness to "tremble" is a kind of selflessness, a process of holding the self's needs in check in the interest of seeing the real. Great art, according to Iris Murdoch, delights us "because we are not used to looking at the real world at all." In her *Metaphysics as a Guide to Morals*, she uses Plato's system of thought to give, ironically, a place to art and the artist that Plato did not envision in *The Republic*. Murdoch argues that the moral life in Plato is a "slow shift of attachments wherein *looking* (concentrating, attending, attentive discipline) is a source of divine (purified) energy. . . . The movement is not, by an occasional leap, into an external (empty) space of freedom, but patiently and continuously a change of one's whole being in all its contingent detail, through a world of appearance toward a world of reality."

We know, of course, that the simple exposure to and even the study of great art may or may not lead to transformation, to care for the other. Art requires our consent, and in Murdoch's view, our "morally disciplined attention" in order to enact the change from "a world of appearance toward a world of reality." What we may learn from art is its closeness to morals, since for Murdoch, the essence of both art and morals is love. And love, as Murdoch defines it in her essay "The Sublime and the Good," "is the extremely difficult realization that something other than oneself is real"; it is the "discovery of reality."

Great art is the enemy of fantasy; fantasy always leads to the creation of idols. Our weakness as human beings is our tendency to make idols of whatever is at hand, whatever makes the world easier, more understandable, and meets our most immediate needs. Poets have always argued that the imagination is the opposite of fantasy. Imagination is an exercise in overcoming one's self, of extending oneself towards what is different from ourselves. And, in their loving respect for a reality other than oneself, imagination and art call us to attend, with devotion and care, to a world which will always remain a mystery, but a mystery in which love calls us to the things of this world where we may become most fully human.

"To Discover an Order as of a Season"
Some Thoughts on Nature Poetry

I'VE BEEN THINKING ABOUT Frost lately, especially his deliberate writing of seemingly old-fashioned verse—nature poetry—to take on modern epistemological and aesthetic questions: questions of how we know and especially the questions of whether poetry imposes or discovers meaning, and all the nuances in between those two poles.

Frost's inheritance was the Puritan tradition in which nature was a book rife with meaning placed by God. The Puritans were confident they could read that book. Of course that confidence had eroded by Frost's time, proving innocent, sometimes absurd, and often violent and harmful. And Frost's poetic father is Wordsworth (it often seems to me that Frost's poems are deliberate re-writings of Wordsworth) who had already probed the world we "half-perceive" and "half-create."

Frost takes a second look at the loss of the Puritan tradition and the possibilities and fears of Romanticism. On the one hand, if we no longer believe that God places meaning in nature, we're free to create our own truth, which is always multiple, as many truths as there are individuals. On the other, such loss can produce anxiety—we're fearful that whatever we create is an imposition of our own needs and will and possibly just another illusion.

In many ways, Wallace Stevens's work—work that is in my mind intimately connected to Frost's—plays out these tensions. Consider his famous poem, "The Idea of Order at Key West," in which a woman walks beside the sea. "She" is the sole arbiter of the world, the poem informs us, who makes the sea sing in her words. And yet the poem poses an oppositional question to this position: would the "She" have any song at all to sing if she were not alongside the sea, if she had not first heard the "meaningless plunges of water and the wind"?

On a larger scale, Stevens's work as a whole plays out the tensions between the imagination as sole creator of meaning and the meaning that is immanent in the world. While "Idea of Order at Key West" is from Stevens's second book, his early work, on the whole, displays the freedom to make meaning that is "unsponsored, free" (see "Sunday Morning"). But his late work makes clear the bondage of the solitary self-generating multiple perspectives, ad infinitum. His search is to discover not to impose. As Stevens says in "Notes Toward A Supreme Fiction, "to discover a reality not our own "is possible, possible, possible. It must be possible." It is this "must" that recognizes what is at stake. Such discovery must be possible if ever we are to escape the inherent loneliness of the solitary self. It is this *must* that forces us out of the "finality of aloneness" (George Steiner's phrase in *Real Presences*) and into speech, and poems.

Nature poetry is an ideal fit for the exploration of these epistemological concerns. Although the nature poem is still as foreign to our modern urban culture as it was in Frost's time, I want to speak about my own sense of the nature poem and why I see the form as particularly apt at addressing the issues of meaning and belief.

I think that my own writing began to take shape when I realized what I believed, what I staked my life on. What I discovered was that, despite the daily atrocities we're witness to, my gut sense of the world was that it was *good*. I use that word as it is used in Genesis: And God looked at the world and saw that it was good. And I use it as a synonym for what Wallace Stevens came to call innocence in the "Auroras of Autumn." Stevens found in that poem that "we are an unhappy people in a happy world." There is a tension, that is, between our daily experience of evil and horror and our ongoing sense of hope.

To me, the oddest, most mysterious aspect of my existence has been the experience of hope proved "along the pulses," as Keats would say. George Steiner has said, the one thing that cannot be deconstructed is hope. And Simone Weil put it this way: "At the bottom of the heart of every human being, from earliest infancy to the tomb, there is something that goes on indomitably expecting, in the teeth of all experience of crimes committed, suffered and witnessed, that good and not evil will be done to him. It is this above all that is sacred in every human being" (Essay on "Human Personality").

At the heart of most nature poems—even if this tenet is called into question—is both the trust and hope that there is some connection between the natural world and the human community. Most nature poems place their trust in attentiveness. Wendell Berry, in an essay from *What*

Are People For writes: "to pay attention is to come into the presence of a subject. In one of its root senses, it is to 'stretch toward' a subject, a kind of aspiration. We speak of 'paying attention' because of a correct perception that attention is owed." Berry's statement is grounded, as are nature poems, in a belief that there is a reality outside our mental universe. And that belief is connected to the structure and language of a nature poem—that is, the poem's artifice of realism and its stance that words are not entirely arbitrary.

Let me turn to Berry again to define what I mean by "not entirely arbitrary." In the title essay of his book *Standing By Words,* Berry defines his "stand"; he writes that "no statement is complete or comprehensible in itself, and that in order for a statement to be complete and comprehensible three conditions are required: it must designate its object precisely; its speaker must stand by it: must believe it, be accountable for it, be willing to act on it; and, finally, this relation of speaker, word, and object must be conventional; the community must know what it is."

One of the communal aspects of traditional nature poems is the walk. A person goes out into the natural world, looks around, and reflects on what is seen. As A. R. Ammons has shown in "Corson's Inlet," the "walk" has a built-in open-endedness about it. Even if we're walking to a specific location, each walk is new because what comes to our attention is constantly changing. Whether it's Frank O'Hara walking the streets of New York noticing "this and that" or Frost coming upon an abandoned woodpile in a frozen swamp, the walk poem invokes both a spatial landscape and the landscape of one's own mind. The sticking point, of course, involves the relationship between the two. I think that the nature poem is a particularly apt vehicle for exploring that relationship.

For me, the best nature poems constantly keep in question the meaning that the mind creates out of its own needs and desires, and that meaning which, while we may never be able to make sense of it, lies outside the mind's powers. We have learned to call into question the dangerous Romantic illusions of self-possession and the dogmas surrounding our capacity to know, to reach any kind of formalizable completeness. But that doesn't cancel what I see as the poet's task: the revelation of presence, an awakening to the astonishing sense that things are, though they need not be. And our modern beliefs don't negate the nature poem's search for a reality and meaning outside the mind's constructions. If anything, such thought intensifies the urgency of and necessity of that search.

Here's Frost's poem "Mowing" as an example:

There was never a sound beside the wood but one,

And that was my long scythe whispering to the ground.
What was it it whispered? I knew not well myself;
Perhaps it was something about the heat of the sun,
Something, perhaps, about the lack of sound—
And that was why it whispered and did not speak.
It was no dream of the gift of idle hours,
Or easy gold at the hand of fay or elf:
Anything more than the truth would have seemed too weak
To the earnest love that laid the swale in rows,
Not without feeble-pointed spikes of flowers
(Pale orchises), and scared a bright green snake.
The fact is the sweetest dream that labor knows.
My long scythe whispered and left the hay to make.

There's no Romantic passive listener here, waiting for the truth of nature to reveal itself. But there is both an attentiveness to the world and the job at hand, and a need to probe the sensed connection between mower, scythe, and swale: "what was it it whispered?" Certainly the question itself, asked of a scythe, commits that old pathetic fallacy of giving human characteristic to a scythe. But Frost purposefully draws our attention to the mind's imposition—to its need to find a meaning in the sound of the swinging scythe; and, perhaps more importantly, he also draws our attention to the way the work's rhythms create an intimacy that is real but quite unexplainable. Consider the syntax of the answer: "What was it it whispered? I knew not well myself." Here's that wonderful Frost-style ambiguity. It could be that the speaker doesn't know very well what it is the scythe whispers. Or he may not know himself very well. And it may be that he's feeling the effects of being taken out of himself and into the sounds of his labor.

After considering the various possibilities, the speaker is certain only of what the sound is not. There will be no easy transcendence here: the sound may be about the sweat of our labor ("the heat of the sun"), but it surely is not some faery truth. No, whatever the sound means, its meaning is only to be found in the "earnest love that laid the swale in rows." The speaker, moving within the rhythms of his mowing and the rhythms of his mind's reflections, comes, in time, to this: "The fact is the sweetest dream that labor knows." The "fact" here, as its Latin origin— *factum*, an "act or feat"—suggests, is the mown hay, that which has been done. But the speaker's satisfaction comes not in the results, but in the labor itself. Whatever is known is known only as the felt sweetness of a moment when some wholeness constellates itself out of the particulars of sweat, swale, consciousness, and scythe. Is this sweet sense of wholeness discovered in nature or imposed by human nature? Frost gives us only the silence of the period between his two final sentences:

> The fact is the sweetest dream that labor knows.
> My long scythe whispered and left the hay to make.

The swale has been cut. It will become hay as it dries in the sun. The speaker has felt the sweetness of his labor. At this border between nature's silence and the speaker's need for meaningful speech, the world of nature and the human world both are joined and kept apart. At this border there is an exchange of gifts—the speaker received nature's self-forgetfulness, and nature, the gift of human consciousness.

Rilke's advice in his *Letters to a Young Poet* is pertinent here; he says to the young poet: "Don't search for answers, which could not be given to you now, because you would be unable to live them. And the point is to live everything. Live the questions now, perhaps, then, someday far in the future, you will gradually, without ever noticing it, live your way into the answer." Knowing, here, comes of living. Knowledge consists both of taking the world into ourselves, and the love of going out to the things of the world themselves.

As Stevens's and Frost's poetry illustrate, there is a need to deconstruct the old hierarchies, to constantly remind ourselves of the mind's endless impositions of meaning; but, to me, the process of doing so is not to end with the "intricate play of / at the surface of language itself" (Charles Bernstein's phrase), but rather in order to

> . . . discover an order as of
> A season, to discover summer and know it,
> To discover winter and know it well, to find,
> Not to impose, not to have reasoned at all,
> Out of nothing to come on major weather . . .
> (Stevens, "Notes Toward a Supreme Fiction")

The nature poem, then, as practiced by the best writers from Wordsworth to Frost to Merwin, Hass, and Charles Wright in our own time, makes use of the built-in tensions between the landscape and the speaker's reflections as he / she moves through that landscape. The best nature poems never arrive at a fictional Eden, are never an escape from the world's horror, but rather are an attempt to register the feel of what is always lost: "the muddy center before we breathed," as Stevens put it in "Notes Toward A Supreme Fiction." Yet if this "muddy center" cannot be reached within the normal operations of language, it still exists beyond our capacity to name it, even if whatever we can know of that "muddy center" arises from our naming and imagining. My point is this: far from being a throwback to some nostalgic past, the contemporary nature poem can have the continuing, and essential value, of reminding us of an origin that cannot be rendered intelligible, that cannot be made our own (we do not create the world), that invokes terror more often than joy, and that can be discovered only as a gift.

And so I arrive at those already mentioned characteristics: that the nature poem operates out of the trust that there is some connection between the natural world and the human community; that paying attention is "owed" because there is a reality outside our mental universe; that words point to something beyond themselves. All poems—regardless of style—move towards (or attempt to) the chaos of our perceptions, the rawness of our experience, and then back again, submitting that chaos to the regularizing mode of language. The difference between the poem, which "means" solely at the level of the surface play of "sound, movement, and energy" (Dean Young's phrase), say, and the nature poem I'm trying to describe, is the wager on meaning I spoke of. The poem I'm looking for and trying to write wagers on meaning even though, as George Steiner has said, we cannot "make final sense of sense itself."

But what grounds this wager on meaning? One such ground is the new biological understanding that we live in a reciprocal and interactive world. Simply put, the ecological model cultivates the insight that everything is connected. To say this can have a kind of new age goofiness—and often does. But the validity of such a statement rests on seeing each thing in its singularity, in its difference from everything else—most of all ourselves—while at the same time realizing that each thing is bound to another in vital relationship.

The best nature poems to my mind do not find a system of symbols in the natural world, but rather a world that stands for nothing but itself, its actual existence an ongoing presentation that is always creating in the present. But if nature lies outside our grasp, it is still the context in which we exist, the context that has made us who we are. In *The Practice of the Wild*, Gary Snyder puts it this way:

> I have a friend who feels sometimes that the world is hostile to human life—he says it chills us and kills us. But how could we be were it not for this planet that provided our very shape? Two conditions—gravity and a liveable temperature range between freezing and boiling—have given us fluids and flesh. The trees we climb and the ground we walk on have given us fluids and flesh. The "place" (from the root *Plat*, broad, spreading, flat) gave us far-seeing eyes, the streams

and breezes gave us versatile tongues and whorly ears. The
land gave us stride, and the lake a dive. The amazement gave
us our kind of mind.

The nature poem I'm trying to describe, then, must recognize the
difference between ourselves and the world, while, at the same time, recognizing that we do not exist as "rootless intelligences without layers of
localized contexts" (Snyder). To quote Snyder again, we must recognize
that "grandparents, place, grammar, pets, lovers, children, tools, the poems and songs we remember, are what we think with."

Here's Robert Hass's both maligned and praised famous poem,
"Meditation at Lagunitas" from his book *Praise*:

All the new thinking is about loss.
In this it resembles all the old thinking.
The idea, for example, that each particular erases
the luminous clarity of a general idea. That the clown-
faced woodpecker probing the dead sculpted trunk
of that black birch is, by his presence,
some tragic falling off from a first world
of undivided light. Or the notion that,
because there is in this world no one thing
to which the bramble of *blackberry* corresponds,
a word is elegy to what it signifies.
We talked about it late last night and in the voice
of my friend, there was a thin wire of grief, a tone
almost querulous. After a while I understood that,
talking this way, everything dissolves: *justice,*
pine, hair, woman, you and *I*. There was a woman
I made love to and I remembered how, holding
her small shoulders in my hands sometimes
I felt a violent wonder at her presence
like a thirst for salt, for my childhood river
with its island willow, silly music from the pleasure boat,
muddy places where we caught a little orange-silver fish
called *pumpkinseed*. It hardly had to do with her.
Longing, we say, because desire is full
of endless distances. I must have been the same to her.
I remember so much, the way her hands dismantled bread,
the thing her father said that hurt her, what
she dreamed. There are moments when the body is as numinous
as words, days that are the good flesh continuing.
Such tenderness, those afternoons and evenings,
saying *blackberry, blackberry, blackberry.*

Hass has woken to the memory of a previous night's conversation with a friend. That conversation concerned loss, specifically those old notions that the particular subtracts from the universal, the actual clownish woodpecker from the Idea of Woodpecker, and the new idea that words point to an absence since the word *blackberry* is not a blackberry but a word, and that word means something different to all of us, depending on who we are, what our experience is with blackberries and so on. In that sense the word is an "elegy to what it signifies."

But then Hass realizes that this kind of abstract talking and these kinds of theories about language make the world "dissolve" and, more importantly to our speaker's reflection, don't correspond with his experience. As the passage from Snyder makes clear, words like *pumpkinseed, bread, woman* are connected to our experience of the place in which we live, and have contexts that are crucial to their meaning (Hass's childhood river, a woman who cut bread in a specific way, the woman he made love to, the feel of her shoulders in his hands). In that sense words are not elegies so much as evocations, belonging to the particulars of experience in which Hass's poem immerses us, so that when *blackberry* is repeated in the last line three times, it evokes the presence of blackberry rather than its absence.

The contemporary nature poem reenacts, it seems to me, what Elizabeth Bishop jokingly calls "total immersion" in her poem "At the Fishhouses." As in Bishop's poems, the details accrue and accrue, literal and accurate, and meaning is evoked through the accumulation of those particulars. Though critics are sometimes right to criticize those poets who move too blithely from the ordinary world to hidden symbolic meanings, unaware it seems of the "oh-so-sensitive" speaking "I" at the center of their lyrical visions, it seems to me they often ignore or simply don't see the probing consciousness that is at home in the "immersion" of details—all those memories of Hass that evoke both our bodies in the world and the way in which words themselves are embodied. In the best nature poems the "meaning" (and by meaning I intend no singular truth) of the poem suggests itself out of the process of discovery—a process taking place between the poet and the world, the poet and the poem, the reader and the poem, and the reader and the world.

The nature poem that I see as vital cannot return to the metaphor of "nature as a book." That way of thinking always returns us to that fundamental dichotomy of self and world. In his essay, "The Noble Rider and the Sound of Words," Wallace Stevens gave this definition of poetry, or what he thought poetry should be: "A revelation in words by means of the words." If our experience is language-bound, as Stevens acknowledges, it still has the capacity to surprise its user, to "refresh life," in Stevens's words.

Nature poems have an obvious advantage, it seems to me, in this task. They use language to turn our attentions to the world—not in order to understand it, but in order to see it. By "refresh" Stevens meant a capacity to see the world as if for the first time, free of what he called the "man-locked set" of our preconceptions.

To Gary Snyder this involves the recognition that human beings didn't get "smarter" at some point and invent first language and then society. For Snyder, "Language and culture emerge from our biological-social natural existence. Animals that we were / are." We cannot take credit for language. It is of a complexity that eludes our intellectual capacities—the linguists go on trying to describe, unsuccessfully, language a child learns and masters by the age of six. And certainly we have all felt some connection between the world and our urge to give its elusiveness a voice in words.

For me, the heart of the nature poem has always been grounded in its need to pronounce—again and again—that the world is and for no reason. The journals of Lewis and Clark, replete with the struggle and urgency to find a language for the expanse and abundance of the world they were confronted by, added over 1,500 words to the American language. Or think of the child's hunger for words—what's this, the child asks, what's this, what's this.

Our mistake has been to think that once something is named that we know it, that chaos has been resolved into order. Modern physics has taught us, thankfully, that each thing is really an event: at the sub-atomic level there is no longer a clear distinction between what is and what happens. The physicist John Wheeler puts it this way: "Nothing is more important about the quantum principle than this, that it destroys the concept of the world as 'sitting out there' with the observer safely separated from it. . . ." The universe is a participatory universe. One, as I suggested earlier, which the poem is constantly trying to be attentive to and present for.

Such attention in the nature poem—and this characteristic is essential—must be passionate and modest simultaneously. A nature poem by definition can only be an account of something too large to grasp. It must be accountable to the strangeness of our existence and the world's. As Wallace Stevens put it,

> From this the poem springs: that we live in a place

That is not our own and, much more, not ourselves
And hard it is in spite of blazoned days.

The nature poem, then, reminds us as well of our constant hubris, our arrogance in thinking that we create the world. It is in this role that I think the nature poem is most spiritual and political. In *Imagining the Earth*, John Elder draws an analogy between wilderness areas and poetry: "In both cases," he writes, "human reason draws and defends a boundary beyond which its own dominance will not be allowed." In reminding us that the non-human is the context for the human, that we must, as John Elder has put it, become "true servants" of the earth, nature poetry is spiritual and political. The best nature poems bring us face to face with the utter strangeness of our existence, with the core of irrationality we cannot comprehend, while reminding us that we still endure. Let me conclude then with a passage from Simone Weil's essay, "The Needs of the Soul":

> The great instigators of violence have encouraged themselves with the thought of how blind forces are sovereign throughout the whole universe. By looking at the world with keener senses we shall find a more powerful encouragement in the thought of how these innumerable blind forces are limited, made to balance one against the other, brought to form a whole by something which we do not understand, but which we call beauty.

The Longest Day

On the In-Betweenness of Art

IT'S 1970. I'M TWENTY-ONE, IN the rare book room of my college library reading Chinese poetry and making notes for a poem—no doubt a bad poem—and yet I am caught up in it entirely. Below, out the library window, in the college's main quadrangle, there is a large protest going on against the Vietnam War. Students are yelling, faculty members challenging each other's beliefs in public, and the whole school debating whether it should shut down early, cancelling the rest of the semester's classes in protest of the Kent State shootings and the Cambodian bombings and occupation.

I'm caught between my personal enjoyment of the poems I've been reading, the poem I'm trying to write, and the world outside my window. And the moment is even more complicated because I'm acutely aware that what I am doing inside the library—reading and writing poems—hardly matters in the historical scope of what is taking place outside.

Fast forward to 1996. I've driven to the National Gallery in Washington, DC to see the Vermeer exhibit. I've come not just because I love Vermeer as a painter, but also because, a few days before, leafing through a *New Yorker*, I was stopped by two small images that had been superimposed over one another: one was the face of Duško Tadic, a Serbian accused of multiple rapes and murders, of supervising the torture of Muslim prisoners, including at one point, of forcing one man to emasculate another with his teeth. The other image was the hauntingly beautiful face of the young girl in the Vermeer painting we know as "The Girl with a Pearl Earring," sometimes referred to as "The Girl in a Turban."

These images, so incongruous, were the lead-in to an article by Lawrence Weschler called "Inventing Peace." The origin of the article was a remark by an Italian jurist on the Yugoslav War Crime Tribunal in Hague. Asked by Weschler how, obliged to listen to and adjudicate atrocities like that of Tadic's each day, he kept from going mad, the Italian judge replied, "as often as possible I make my way over to the museum to spend a little time with the Vermeers."

Now one might conclude that the judge simply found a respite in Vermeer's oriental rugs or those lush, velvety folds of curtains and dresses. Or in those moments of human life when, absorbed in the act of writing a letter or pouring milk or weighing pearls, we enter the rhythms of shifting light that falls through a casement window. But for the judge, Vermeer's achievement resided in the way the painter invented a "zone filled with peace, a small room, an intimate vision" at a turbulent juncture in history when the geography of the Netherlands, the distribution of Protestants and Catholics, and threats from both the English and French, were being sorted out and contested.

We might say that Vermeer's curtains, dresses, windows, and oriental rugs, all manifest the order that is already there, in things as they are. Not the order we think should be there, but the one that is. I don't mean to suggest that Vermeer did not choose to apply a thin glaze of blue paint over a base of reddish brown so that a plaster wall seems to radiate its own inner light. Up close, of course, the threads of the oriental rug reveal themselves as thin, brushed lines of white paint, and surely a wooden table was placed perpendicular to the picture frame to achieve a compositional balance.

But I do mean to suggest that the serenity of Vermeer's work always seems to lie in Vermeer's refusal to privilege one thing over another. Vermeer inherited the epic tradition of history paintings and the already culturally determined idea of what subject matter was appropriate to that tradition. His great strength was to reside in the in-between of his paintings, looking away from what society had learned to see so that he might look at the specific individual in those moments that make up our everyday lives. Intimacy and distance: Vermeer makes an accurate report of both and, in doing so, invents the peace that both Weschler and the Italian judge find so dear.

Chinese poetry and Vermeer: two moments, twenty-six years apart. What links these two moments is the tension between one's responsibility to the personal demands of making art and to the social world one shares with others. As writers, we are always in conversation with the world we live in, whether or not we write directly or indirectly about the events of our day. Eavan Boland, the Irish poet and essayist, notes "who the poet is, what he or she nominates as the proper theme for poetry, what self they discover and confirm through their subject matter—all of this involves an ethical choice."

True enough. Poetry is an act which gathers and shapes, which looks for wholeness, even as our daily experience is continuously shattered against what Wallace Stevens called the "pressure of reality." If, as Stevens says, the pressure of reality is always a force of disintegration and self-division—the sufferings and sorrows which daily cross our path—then poetry must be an equal and counterbalancing force, the acts of the imagination pushing back against the pressure of reality. And yet if "reality calls for a name, for words," as Czeslaw Milosz put it, we also know, as Milosz knew all too well, when that reality draws too close, the "poet's mouth cannot even enter a complaint of Job: all art proves to be nothing compared with action." Poetry, of course, as Auden said, "makes nothing happen." It cannot stand in the way of political and historical encroachments.

But I do believe poetry makes something happen. So did Auden. The line I quoted from Auden is almost always quoted out of context. It appears in Auden's elegy for Yeats, written in 1939, in a time when nations were gearing up for World War II, "each sequestered in its hate," as the poem puts it. In the section of the poem where the line about poetry making nothing happen appears, Auden considers how "mad Ireland" "hurt" Yeats into poetry and how, now that Yeats is dead, Ireland's madness continues. In that context, "poetry makes nothing happen." But there is a too often forgotten colon after the word "happen" and what follows in this section and the next is an explanation of what poetry *does* make happen. Consider:

> For poetry makes nothing happen: it survives
> In the valley of its making, where executives
> Would never want to tamper, flows on south
> From ranches of isolation and the busy griefs,
> Raw towns that we believe and die in; it survives,
> A way of happening, a mouth.

Auden's poem continues, in its next section, to advise poets in the voice and meter of Yeats's "Under Ben Bulben," to

> Follow, poet, follow right
> To the bottom of the night,
> With your unconstraining voice
> Still persuade us to rejoice,
>
> With the farming of a verse,

Make a vineyard of the curse,
Sing of human unsuccess
In a rapture of distress,

In the deserts of the heart
Let the healing fountain start,
In the prison of his days,
Teach the free man how to praise.

In context, the often-quoted line about what poetry cannot do, helps delineate what poetry can do, must do even. If we ask poetry to stop a bullet, to feed the hungry, yes, it can do nothing. Perhaps poems only "survive" because the people that "matter"—executives who wield and deal power and money and people's lives—pay it no attention. Or perhaps these executives never want to enter what Auden calls the "valley of poetry's making"—a valley where for Auden the poet holds up a mirror to the self—and struggles to "make a vineyard of the curse." As Auden knew, poetry cannot make us good, but it can prevent us from imagining that we already are. John F. Kennedy, speaking in honor of Robert Frost at Amherst College in 1963 shortly before his own death, said quite powerfully, "When power leads men towards arrogance, poetry reminds him of his limitations. When power narrows the areas of man's concern, poetry reminds him of the richness and diversity of his existence."

But how does poetry (and art, in general, of course) create such transformations? In the title essay of Seamus Heaney's book, *The Government of the Tongue,* Heaney gives us a parable about poetry; it's based on a familiar parable from the Gospel of John. In the Gospel narrative, the Pharisees bring a woman who was caught in the act of adultery before Jesus. The Pharisees say the woman must be stoned according to the law commanded by Moses. Jesus does not answer the Pharisees when they ask him for his judgment. Instead he writes with his finger on the ground. When the Pharisees persist with their questions, Jesus responds, "He that is without sin among you, let him cast a stone at her," and goes on writing in the dirt.

Here is Seamus Heaney's inspired response:

> The drawing of those characters is like poetry, a break with the usual life, but not an absconding from it. Poetry, like the writing, is arbitrary and marks time in every possible sense of that phrase. It does not say the accusing word or say to the helpless accused, 'Now a solution will take place'; it does not propose to be instrumental or effective. Instead, in the

rift between what is going to happen and whatever we would
wish to happen, poetry holds attention for a space, functions
not as distraction but as pure concentration, a focus where
our power to concentrate is concentrated back on ourselves.

As the executives and the nations were in Auden's poem, the members of the crowd in John's parable are convicted by their own conscience. The accusers of the adulterous woman—you and I and each of us who say "This is someone whom I am better than"—are forced by Christ's silent writing to reflect back on their own moral position.

Poems, then, are like Christ's writing in the dirt—they can create an interval where cause and effect logic is suddenly undermined. In that interval, the writing's very lack of moral judgment is its morality, a morality that changes the direction of the Pharisees and brings them face-to-face with the individual woman who is standing before them. The woman must be responded to not as a type—adulteress—but as someone worthy of their fullest human response. That is what poetry makes happen: poems create that interval in which we can see the very fullness of our existence; or, to say it another way, poems create a space in which it is possible to turn away from the dim, reductive hearts inside us.

I want, now, to look a little harder at that interval which Heaney called a "rift" in our usual thinking. I just said that the very lack of moral judgment in that rift or interval is writing's morality. Keats famously said that the best poems have "Negative Capability"—he was trying at the time to define great achievement in art, especially in literature (Keats wanted, quite simply, to define the quality which made Shakespeare, Shakespeare). Negative Capability, Keats said, occurs when a person is "capable of being in uncertainties, mysteries, doubts, without any irritable reaching after fact and reason."

What Heaney called a "rift," what Keats called "Negative Capability," I'm defining as in-betweeness, a word I am borrowing from my friend and colleague at Holy Cross, James Kee, who informs me that he found the idea of the "in-between" in Eric Voegelin who, in turn, was working on Plato's use of the preposition "between" in the dialogues.

I'm using the word "in-betweenness" because I want to suggest that in-betweenness is the condition of our humanness. We live between our birth and death, about which we can know almost nothing. And in between our birth and death, we try, simultaneously, to make sense of the unexplainable, terrifying, and painful aspects of human experience as well as the intrinsic joy of being. The tools we have to make sense of these contradictions are, on the one hand, the demystification that a necessary deconstructive self-consciousness brings to bear, and, on the other, an openness to the mystery that consciousness can never represent or master. Our life, as the philosopher Simone Weil knew so well, takes place on the cross of these contradictions.

So, too, I am arguing, does poetry, and art in general. The poem, as Wallace Stevens, has said, must exist, "in the difficulty of what it is to be." Part of the "difficulty of what it is to be" has to do with how hard it is for the writer to capture what Anne Carson, the classicist and poet, calls an "understanding of what life feels like." Reality, by its very nature, remains extraordinarily complex and opaque. As Vaclav Havel has written: "Spirit, the human soul, our self-awareness, our ability to generalize and think in concepts, to perceive the world as the world (and not just our locality) and lastly, our capacity for knowing that we will die—and living in spite of that knowledge—surely all these are mediated or actually created by words."

As word users, Havel subsequently points out, we have tried "incessantly to address that which is concealed by mystery, and influence it with our words. As believers we pray to God . . . as people who belong to modern civilization—whether believers or not—we use words to construct scientific theses and political ideologies with which to tackle or redirect the course of history—successfully or otherwise."

Note Havel's use of the word "influence": we want to influence that which is concealed by mystery with our words. For Havel the power of words is neither unambiguous nor clear-cut. Words can compel us with their freedom and truthfulness and they can deceive us, madden us. Havel's warning about words is simple and direct: it pays to be suspicious of words, to be wary of them since "the same word can be true at one moment and false the next, at one moment illuminating, at another deceptive."

So what is the writer to do? In her wonderful essay, "The Sublime and the Good," Iris Murdoch reminds us that when Shelley said that "egotism was the great enemy of poetry," he meant that writing is an exercise in overcoming one's self, in attending to something "quite particular other than oneself." As such, art's greatest enemy is fantasy, since fantasy constantly deforms the reality we are sunk in. Instead of attending to reality, it is easier for us to deform it, to create theories and explanations that give us a kind of control of its mystery and, in turn, make us monarchs of all we survey.

Our task, then, as writers/artists is to make the real world as real as possible, to paraphrase Gary Snyder. To overcome fantasy, egotism, and solipsism requires love, according to Murdoch. She defines love this way: "Love is the extremely difficult realization that something other than oneself is real." But for Murdoch love entails a tragic freedom. The tragic freedom is this: "we all have an infinitely extended capacity to imagine the being of others. Tragic, because there is no prefabricated harmony, and others are, to an extent we never cease discovering, different from ourselves. Nor is there any social totality within which we come to comprehend differences as placed and reconciled. We have only a segment of the circle."

Yes, we have only our in-betweenness, our segment of the circle, from which we must keep imagining the circle. In a poem of my own called "Czeslaw Milosz's Glasses," I say about Milosz that "he knew words / could never navigate the roundness of things. / and yet knew, too, that his work was to catch / the complexity of all in one unwritable sentence / he tried to write again and again."

If art is an act of attention, that attention necessarily involves an act of love, an act which we can only extend out of our in-betweenness— that is, the infinite extension of imaginative understanding towards that which remains irreducible in its otherness and yet open to our understanding and recognition.

In-betweenness. The Saturday between Good Friday and Easter. At the end of his book, *Real Presences*, George Steiner writes:

> There is one particular day in Western history about which neither historical record nor myth nor Scripture make report. It is Saturday. And it has become the longest of days. We know of that Good Friday which Christianity holds to have been that of the Cross. But the non-Christian, the atheist, knows of it as well. This is to say that he knows of injustice, of the interminable suffering, of the waste, of the brute enigma of ending, which so largely make up not only the historical condition, but the everyday fabric of our personal lives. . . . We also know about Sunday. To the Christian, that day signifies an intimation, both assured and precarious, both evident and beyond comprehension. . . . If we are non-Christians or non-believers we conceive of that day as the day of liberation from inhumanity and servitude. . . . But ours is the long day's journey of that Saturday.

Steiner knows that in the face of the countless inhumanities that take place, all art is helpless. But he also knows that without the figurations of art, which tell again and again of our sorrows and our pains as well as our hopes and happiness, we could not wait and wait. The artists' responsibility is to Saturday. To want the certainty of Good Friday or Easter would be, an "irritable reaching after fact and reason," as Keats said. But on that longest of days, the artist must make the most accurate report he or she can muster, not because the artist is in search of what Milosz mockingly calls the "golden fleece of a perfect form," but because the artist's report is as necessary as love and is the only way we have of balancing the violence of reality.

I was just a confused, bad poet as I sat in that library room some forty years ago. But I knew poetry's magic; I knew words gave the world life and the "savor it possesses," as Stevens once said. And I knew poems had to confront those events that are beyond our power to tranquilize. This is not to say that those events are the same for everyone or even that certain subjects should demand a writer's attention. But it is to say that poetry is a counterbalance, an act which gathers and shapes and looks for the "whole" when we are confronted with the forces of disintegration and self-division.

The writer must learn to live "in-between"—he or she must be part deconstructionist, "wresting the past from fiction and legends" (a phrase of Milosz's) so that things may be described as they are, and part fabulist so that what is seen and described is recreated in the imagination and becomes, as Wallace Stevens put it, "a revelation in words by means of words."

When we hear those words, they must come to us as a need fulfilled. Wallace Stevens, Vermeer, Auden, Milosz, and Seamus Heaney all insist on art's power to "redress" (Heaney's word). Though the title of Heaney's famous essay, "The Redress of Poetry," uses the word redress in its usual sense as a noun, Heaney's interest is clearly in the suggestions of redress as a verb.

In this time when poetry, and art in general, is too often viewed as merely a reflection of the power structures that produced it, when poems are too often praised or criticized solely for their politics, Heaney rightly insists on poetry's power to redress—that is, "to set a person or thing upright again." Heaney explains how this setting upright occurs, when he writes, "I want to celebrate [poetry's] given, unforeseeable thereness, the way it enters our field of vision and animates our physical and intelligent being in much the same way as the birds shapes stenciled on the transparent surfaces of glass walls or window must suddenly enter the vision and change the direction of the real bird's flight."

Poems must know the "nightmare of the dark," as Auden named it, but the poem's work is always to free us from the curse of being locked inside of our own self-isolation. The poems we turn to induce a "swerve" in us; they change the direction of our flight not by telling us where to go, but by transmitting the "thereness" of the world to us; in doing so, they create an interval in which we might choose the light of justice and the goodness of the cosmos, even if we live in darkness, and know that darkness as part of ourselves.

The Revolt Against Narcissus

We find comfort only in another beauty, in others' music, in the poetry of others. Salvation lies with others, though solitude may taste like opium.

> —"Another Beauty," Adam Zagajewski

IN A SCENE FROM BOOK IV of Milton's *Paradise Lost*, Adam and Eve talk one evening of the glories of Eden and their unmerited free creation by God, unaware that they are being watched by Satan. This little scene takes place shortly after Satan's shape-shifting arrival in Eden and serves as a kind of foreshadowing of Eve's later temptation in Book IX.

As Eve is recalling the moment when she woke into life after her creation, she remembers that there was a very small interval of time between her waking and the moment when God brought her to meet Adam for the first time. In that interval, Eve, waking to the sound of water, traces the sound to a cave and from the cave to a little lake. As in Ovid's tale of Narcissus, from which Milton is clearly borrowing, Eve bends over the still water and sees what she calls a "Shape" within the "watery gleam." The reflection mirrors her actions and she is immediately delighted by what she takes as "answering looks of sympathy and love." So delighted in fact that Eve tells Adam how she would have "fixed" her eyes on that image alone and "pin'd with vain desire" if a voice had not broken into her reverie. The voice, of course, is God's who tells Eve that the shape she sees in the water is herself, a reflection that merely comes and goes with Eve. In place of that self-reflection, God will bring Eve to Adam within whom she can truly see herself.

This little scene contains a number of essential ideas in Milton's epic tale and offers us some day-to-day practical wisdom. First, Milton suggests how quickly and essentially we see the world through our own false conceptions of it. Immediately upon waking in the world, Eve, bending over the lake water, thinks the "shape" she sees there offers her sympathy and love, though she is only seeing her own love for herself. Here's our original sin even before Eve and Adam have eaten from the Tree of Knowledge—that we think we know more than we know, or can know. And, while current psychology and common sense tell us that we must love ourselves in order to love others, Milton's point is more subtle: we only truly know our face in the face of the other. God, remember, tells Eve that the reflection she sees in the water will depart with her and return when she returns to the lake. Good science, certainly, but Milton's metaphor here is crucial: the self we see in the mirror is not truly our self. Eve's happiness cannot be found by seeing her reflected image in Adam's eyes; nor can Adam's happiness be found in his reflection in Eve's eyes. But Eve's love for Adam can be seen by Adam in Eve's face. And so can Eve know Adam's love, truly see herself in that love, in Adam's face. To believe that the reflected shape is truly ourselves is, in Milton, to damn ourselves. Throughout *Paradise Lost,* the face of evil is the contracted image of the self gazing at itself. It is Satan reducing the world to his own mind.

Place this scene from Milton against a contemporary reimagining of the Narcissus's myth that appears in a book of his own poetry, *Parables and Portraits,* by Stephen Mitchell, who is more widely known for his excellent translations. Mitchell's little prose poem goes like this:

> It was not the image of his own face that transfixed him as he bent down over the pool. He had seen that face often before: in mirrors, in a thousand photographs, in women's eyes. It was an undistinguished face, but handsome enough, with long eyelashes, full lips, stately nose sloping to a curious plateau above the lip. No, it was something else now that rooted him to the spot. Kneeling there, gazing into the so-taken-for-granted form, he grew more and more poignantly aware that it was mere surface. When the water was calm, it was calm. When the water rippled at the touch of a leaf or fish, it too rippled; or broke apart when he churned the water with his hand. More and more fascinated, he kept staring through the image of his face into the depths beneath, filled with a multitude of other, moving, shadowy forms. He knew that if he stayed there long and patiently enough, he would

be able to see straight through to the bottom. And at that moment, he knew, the image would disappear.

Mitchell's Narcissus has realized, as Eve did not but as we all must sooner or later, that the self-image rippling on the water is "mere surface." As God warned Eve, that image departs with her; it is dictated by the surrounding conditions—wind, a leaf falling, a hand breaking the watery image. In Mitchell's tale, Narcissus learns to stare through that image of his face into the depths beneath, filled with a "multitude of other, moving, shadowy forms." The crucial word here is "other." The multitude of shadowy forms is more fascinating and more absorbing than himself (even if we concede that the self is still doing the looking and is seeing those forms, perhaps, in terms of some relationship to the self).

Mitchell goes a step further: even more important than what Narcissus sees is what he comes to believe: "He knew that if he stayed there long and patiently enough he would be able to see straight through to the bottom . . . he knew the image would disappear." Time, patience, and attention to those "other" forms are all necessary if the watery image of the self is to be seen through. I remember reading Ruskin's *Modern Painters* during my first year of graduate studies. Making a case for the literal truth of Turner's paintings, Ruskin pointed out how, because Turner is a literally-accurate painter of water, we *either* see the surface of water *or* we see through the surface to what lies underneath. But we cannot see the surface and the bottom simultaneously—just as in those gestalt drawings of the two faces in profile, we can see the two faces or the vase those two faces make. My point is simple: we cannot see life if we're looking at our reflections. To escape what the poet Wallace Stevens called the "man-locked set" of our predispositions and doctrines and see "straight through to the bottom" is to learn how to be "rooted" "to the spot" as Mitchell puts it in his parable of Narcissus.

Given the fact that I am a writer and have spent half my life teaching literature, especially poetry, what I have to say next will come as no surprise. For me, literature and our reading of literature are places where we can take "root." In an article for the *New Republic,* Mario Vargas Llosa, argues that our era of specialized knowledge, brought on by the development of science and technology, increasingly requires an arcane and specialized language. We know the benefits certainly of such specialization—the rapid advances in medicine, in the transfer of information around the world, in the extension of our own life spans. But we are not always aware of the costs—in Llosa's words, the "elimination of common intellectual and cultural traits that permit men and women to co-exist, to communicate, to feel a sense of solidarity." Literature, for Llosa, is "one of the common denominators of human experience through which human beings may recognize themselves and converse with each other, no matter how different their professions, their life plans, their geographical and cultural locations, their personal circumstances." To put Llosa's language into the language I have been using, we might say that literature helps us see past our reflections; it helps us to see the world outside ourselves that is too often masked by ourselves.

But merely reading literature will not accomplish these enormously important and life-preserving goals. Certainly the hyper-educated Nazi regime put the lie to that idea. What I want to explore is not simply reading, but what I see as constituting the act of reading and, by extension, the act of writing. Northrop Frye, from whom I take the title of this essay, said that "all reading begins in the revolt against Narcissus." For Frye, the "revolt" is against reading which confirms what we already know or want to be true. (The Bible is the focus of Frye's last three books—*The Great Code, Words with Power*, and *The Double Vision*; for Frye the Bible, and the Trickster God we find there, forces us to separate our "human mirror of God from God's reality").

The experience of reading that Frye speaks of takes us out of our usual position of mastery over words and things and re-situates us in an attitude of listening. All good literature poses unanswerable yet necessary questions about the world we live in. It asks us to consider the fickleness of life, the mystery of love, the monsters that lie within us, the pervasiveness of injustice, the inescapability of death. But as Frye and Llosa understand, "Literature says nothing to those human beings who are satisfied with their lot, who are content with life as they now live it."

I don't mean to imply that reading literature well requires years of graduate training. I'd be the first to admit that my own discipline—literary studies—has done incredible harm to the act of reading over the last twenty years. The belief that good literature has the power to help us past our shallow prejudices and political opinions by reminding us of the complexity and mystery of human existence seems to have disappeared from most college and university English departments. Now one set of politics replaces another.

We've learned, certainly, to look at texts as cultural constructs and to see the all-too-human interests that lie concealed behind the words. And we no longer come to literature with the naïve assumption that the great work is a direct road to some higher truth. But literary theory has almost become a parody of itself in its great relativist leveling: the critic is as important as the author; the reader is as important as the author; there really is no author at all since the reader and critic are as much a part of a work's "meaning" as the author's intentions and, besides, there really is no such thing as originality since words belong to no one in particular and are merely being endlessly rearranged by writers. And what we call literature is no more than the bourgeois discourse of whoever happens to be in power; and all those ideals that make life worth living—love, compassion, justice—are really illusory and sentimental. And so on and so on.

The result, I'm saddened to say, is the professional study of texts and the subsequent loss of why anyone would care about literature at all. In one of the best analyses I have read of this phenomena, David Bosworth points out, in an essay published in the *Georgia Review* entitled "Echo and Narcissus: The Fearful Logic of Postmodern Thought," that our present fate is that of Echo and Narcissus: "the one unable to express herself, the other unable to see beyond himself."

Bosworth's essay contains some truly piercing psychological insights:

- that the primary drive of the postmodern personality, which appears so liberated, is actually one of censorship as can be seen in our present art's favorite strategies and postures: parody, opacity, word play, the hip ironic tone that proclaims the weariness of having seen it all and done it all before; the sense that all emotions and ideals must be undercut.

- that our claim that "language can only refer to itself and that there is no objective reality" leads us unwittingly into Satan's dilemma in *Paradise Lost*. That is, we are insisting that the mind is "its own place."

- that, most poignantly of all, this withdrawal into the mind's own place does not give us the mastery over life we wish for. In fact, as Bosworth says quite eloquently, when we "constrict what we know instead of mapping what exists, we defuse our immediate anxiety at the expense of an eventual effectiveness." Parody, of course, is also a means of hiding. When we convince others that we are in the "know," we hide safely in our knowingness. We are safe, that is, from the anxiety of our feelings and from choosing the apt words for those feelings.

Such safety is precisely what keeps us locked inside the cave of our minds. We need to admit straight away that the insufficiency of our knowledge—the whipping post of theory—has always been our condition. In fact, the Greeks understood such insufficiency as the tragedy of the human condition. Such an admittance is a place to begin. It should never be a negation of the search for truth, if what we mean by truth has something to do with experience as opposed to propositions and logical positions and counter-positions. The French poet and critic, Yves Bonnefoy, asks this question: "What are the subtleties of language, after all, even turned upside down in a thousand different ways, next to the perception one can have, directly, mysteriously, of the movement of leaves against the sky, or the noise fruit makes when it falls into the grass?"

To exit the cave of our minds, to see past the watery reflection of ourselves, requires an interest in, as Flannery O'Connor once put it, what we don't understand rather than what we do. The imaginative act that gives rise to great art and to the act of reading which is a "revolt against Narcissus" requires us to leave our personalities behind and to inhabit another's experience.

The critic Norman Finkelstein, writing about George Steiner's book, *Real Presences*, notes that the "experiencing of the work of created form, is a meeting between two freedoms—the freedom of the work, which in its 'absolute gratuitousness' has spontaneously come into being out of nothing; and the freedom of the recipients, who must willingly open themselves to the work's salutations." The act of reading is an act of love, a going out of one's nature, a sympathetic identification with the mystery of the other, whether the other is a neighbor, a stranger, or God. We love, as Plato saw, what we do not possess.

The act of reading I'm trying to speak of is a revolt against Narcissus because it demands what Simone Weil called attention, as opposed to will. Attention, which Weil saw, incidentally, as the highest goal of education, comprises both the attitude of waiting, as in prayer, and the deprivation, as Weil puts it, of all that I call "I." When we attend to a text we give it all of our attention, giving up in the process, the needs of what Czeslaw Milosz called our "tiny, tiny myness."

I want to call on Luther for a moment. The way Luther said we should read Scripture applies to what I'm saying about how we should read works of literature. Luther argues first and foremost that Scripture does not tolerate the division of letter and spirit. Spirit here means something like a state of living in God's Spirit, as opposed to an intellectual state wherein we conceptually agree with what the text says. Luther's revolutionary idea—that he did not wish to understand Scripture by his spirit or others' but solely by *its* spirit—suggests that Scripture, and literature in general, are not objects of understanding from which we extract meanings. In Luther the reader is not so much the interpreter—that understanding of Luther falsifies him entirely—as the interpreted.

Allen Grossman applies the same hermeneutics in his *Summa Lyrica,* when he writes that "the interpretation of a text ends up in the self-interpretation of a subject, who henceforth understands himself better." Luther's great reform is this: one must encounter the Bible in the spirit in which it was written, an encounter that is not concerned with deciphering a text's meanings but with the experience of the interpretation itself. Scripture must be experienced. As opposed to the idea of a text as a purely analytical object on which interpretation is done, Luther posits a text that inscribes itself in the reader. The experience that Luther speaks of, then, takes the reader out of the usual position of mastery.

Such an experience might be seen in the book of Genesis. In chapter 32, Jacob "wrestles with an angel." As you may remember, Jacob's name in Hebrew can mean deceiver, serpent. Jacob, of course, has demonstrated his aptitude for deception earlier in this story—he has manipulated his older brother Esau for his birthright; and he has pretended to be Esau in order to steal his blessing from their blind father, Isaac. Throughout this story, Jacob, who carries the blessing of Abraham, his grandfather, has become—in his manipulations, in his craftiness and control—the greatest impediment to that blessing's fulfillment. In fact, there can be no peace for Jacob or his family until he confronts his past and achieves some kind of reconciliation with his brother Esau.

At the border of Canaan, then, Jacob, who has come back to his homeland and to meet with his brother, must first wrestle with a stranger. The wrestling match takes place at the Jabbok Ford which Jacob will rename Peniel, or "face of God." A mysterious stranger comes to Jacob in the night and wrestles with him all night long. What can we make of that wrestling?—surely Jacob is wrestling with a number of things: his marriage, his brother, his darkest impulses, God himself, who is so impossible to make sense of (remember this whole tale begins when, Jacob, who is supposed to inherit the promise to Abraham is born seconds after his brother Esau, thus setting off the need, at least in Jacob's mind, for all his manipulations). As Jacob wrestles, he asks for the name of his protagonist, but gets no answer. What he does get is a touch on the thigh that lames him for life. But Jacob will not let go; he clings all night long to his protagonist, asking for a blessing. Though the protagonist is at one point referred to as a "man," he is clearly no man, and, as the story reaches its climax, it's hinted that Jacob has been wrestling with God himself. Finally, while Jacob never learns who he has been wrestling with, he is transformed by divine power into Israel (the word Israel in Hebrew means one who strives with God), and the starting point of God's people.

Like the mysterious stranger with whom Jacob wrestles, then, all readers of this story are forced to wrestle in order to make some sense out of the mystery of existence, out of the never-able-to-be-seen or understood face of God. Like Jacob, we cannot master our situation, which is always one of partial darkness. We cannot control the people around us, including our own families. In fact, the best we can do is precisely what Jacob does: give up control, wrestle with our darkness, and fight for—at the cost of our maiming—a moment of insight, an experience of the unknowable divinity.

I want to look now at a slightly more extended example of what I've been calling the "revolt against Narcissus." As a paradigm of my ideal reader engaged in an act of reading, I want to offer Shakespeare's Hamlet. Hamlet, of course, must wrestle with his father's ghost, his mother's hasty remarriage to his uncle, the likely murderer of his father, and, most of all, with the "rotten" state of Denmark itself where what appears to be is never what is, and where a man's words have been unhinged from his actions.

I'd like you to put aside for a moment all those interpretations of *Hamlet* you have in your head. I'd like to begin with a very simple assertion: that at the end of act 1, after Hamlet has first seen his father's ghost, what Hamlet almost condescendingly and dismissively says to Horatio— "There are more things in heaven and earth, Horatio, / Than are dreamt of in your philosophy"—is precisely what Hamlet will be forced to learn.

The irony here is that Hamlet knows the intellectual truth of his statement but he has never experienced that commonplace truth "flooding his whole soul, like a revelation," as Simone Weil put it. He thinks—mistakenly—that he can get at the truth through a mastering of his situation. He will during the course of the play: "put on an antic disposition," acting mad in order to unmask the madness around him; outthink and outmock everyone that tries to "play him like a flute"; and stage a play for the hard, "scientific" evidence of guilt he is looking for in Claudius. Kenneth Branagh's *Hamlet,* in all its wonderful brash intelligence and manic wordplay (rather than the usual brooding melancholic Hamlet), catches this aspect of *Hamlet* just right to my mind. Yet all these actions get Hamlet nowhere. In fact, these very thought-out actions lead Hamlet to mistake Polonius for Claudius, and subsequently to stab

Polonius; and they help to drive Ophelia to suicide and, finally, Laertes to revenge.

It is not until Hamlet returns—"naked" as he says or born again—from his sea voyage that he begins to experience the truth of his statement to Horatio. Hamlet has been saved—serendipitously by a pirate ship's raid on the ship that was carrying him to England—and when he approaches the graveyard at the beginning of act 5 we see a new man, one who has learned, as Hamlet will explain in the next scene, that only when "our deep plots do pall" do we have the chance to see how "there's a divinity that shapes our ends / Rough-hew them how we will."

Hamlet has finally come to see that he cannot control everything and everyone around him—his "deep plots" are as doomed as Claudius's determined life. As the pun on "will" implies, all those actions which we will, all those decisions that are shaped by our own needs and desires, can, for better or worse, only rough in our lives. The real work of fine carpentry can only occur when we "let be." In a way Hamlet, like Ophelia, has drowned. He has given up his faith in reason. All through the play we have seen him troubled by his doubts, by a need for certainty where there could be none. Now, at the near cost of his own life, Hamlet has entered a realm of experience that only death makes known. There are indeed "more things in heaven and earth / Than are dreamt of in [our] philosophies."

Hamlet's comments in the graveyard scene are his last on the discrepancy between appearance and reality. Death forces Hamlet to see reality as it really is: that our station in life, our particular economic class, our intelligence and training—all are illusory. Death is the great equalizer and should make us ask not what did he or she do but rather what kind of person was this? What was the quality of life that was lived? Hamlet has looked into the face of death and faced his darkest fears—he cannot know what he wants to know; he cannot control the lives of all around him; he cannot force life to be as he would like it to be. He can only face his own radical contingency and the mess his own "deep plots" have strewn about him; he can only accept his own part in the death of a woman whom he loved; he can only be "ready" ("readiness" is indeed "all") to act responsibly and with his whole being in the faithfulness of knowing that we cannot shape our "ends." As St. Anselm might have put it, Hamlet learns that faith is always seeking understanding.

In my little paradigm of Hamlet as ideal reader, you can see, hopefully, that if it is our obligation to use all the training at our disposal to make sense of the words before us, then it is also our obligation to let those words question us. Real reading begins at that moment. Only after Hamlet lets go of his need to control the un-understandable world around him is he granted a measure of understanding. We undergo as readers the same purgatorial experience Hamlet undergoes. In Denmark, nothing is ever one thing; neither is it in literature. Has a character in literature ever been less pinned down than Hamlet? Don't we think we understand him only to have him evade our every definition of him? And isn't it precisely that evasion that forces the experience of his plight upon us?

We attend to Hamlet's every word because those words bring us, again and again, to a place where we experience what the words do not say: "If it be now, 'tis not to come; if it be not to come, it will be now; if it be not now, yet it will come. The readiness is all. . . . Let be." We can footnote this sentence, parse its grammar, apply its general idea to the play as a whole as well we should. But we cannot contain the baffling mystery of those repetitions of "now" and "to come," the effect of all those verb forms that seem to bring present and future to a point of convergence, as in the gospel's always-here always-coming kingdom of God.

We cannot begin to experience those words until we wrestle with the play's most difficult moment: what happens to Hamlet between act 4 and act 5? Does he give up and only turn more passive and suicidal? Or does he have a revelation of the divinity behind our lives and finally accept the mystery of existence on its own mysterious terms as I have suggested? Or is this simply a failed play for whatever reason we want to give? There are, of course, no definitive answers to these questions. But we answer them each time we give ourselves over to the play, each time we let the play interpret us, if only for the duration of our reading.

I want to conclude by asking one last question: how does the act of reading help us become better poets? Certainly one of my unstated premises has been that we can only write as well as we can read, though, as I hope you have seen by now, "reading" to me involves more than what we do with books. For me, "reading" presupposes, as Allen Grossman says, "a meditative sorting of the true situation of the self from false versions." To sort out these versions, we need to write, just as we need to read, against that which we already know.

As with reading, impatience is our enemy. Impatient readers read themselves and their experience (whether it is relevant or not) into what they read in a way that confirms what they already believe. When Abraham raises a knife above his son Isaac, the impatient reader either dismisses the story out of hand or dutifully concludes we should do God's will, or assigns the story to some historical framework whereby the action simply belongs to old sacrificial rites, or concludes, perhaps, that Abraham's God is not our God.

But to come to some understanding of God, we must let the story question us. We must suffer Abraham's decision with him. When we write, we should become a question to ourselves. John Keats called for Negative Capability—the poet, he felt, should exist in a kind of in-between state without trying to foreclose the contradictions he finds himself in or, as Keats puts it, "without any irritable reaching out after fact and reason." His odes, both individually and as a sequence, constantly place Keats in between conflicting truths: between a Grecian Urn's glimpse of unchanging Beauty and the finite, ever-changing, difficult, and fulfilling love of human beings; or between the song of a nightingale that offers an "easeful" death and the difficult act of living in a world of "weariness" and "fret." Keats's poems constantly examine his own desire to live in a world of fantasy and imagination. And the strength and majesty of those poems are directly connected to the rigor and faithfulness of those self-examinations. In her 1996 Nobel prize speech, the Polish poet, Wislawa Szymborska, said that three little words formed the beginning of everything she wrote. Those three words were: I don't know.

For me, poems grow by questioning. Wallace Stevens's famous definition of poetry as an "act of the mind finding what will suffice" suggests the restless nature of great poems. I have always felt that the most important legacy of the Modernist poets was precisely that searching, "ever-restless" mind which posits a truth one moment and then, in the next moment, says, as Eliot does in the *Four Quartets* "That was a way of putting it—not very satisfactory." And then he starts over, looking for another way of putting it. Poetry as self-revision: something I'm sure Eliot learned from his study of seventeenth-century poetry. George Herbert, one of my favorite poets, writes poems that are always correcting the self's misconceptions as Herbert learns to quiet his own voice and listen for the way God speaks.

The goal is never simply to play with alternatives, but rather, a means of sorting, as Grossman put it, the "true situation of the self from false versions." Or, to put it another way, our obligation as writers is always to distinguish, as Allen Grossman notes in *The Sighted Singer*, "between what is real and what is only desired." The great mistake, I've lately come to see in my writing of poems and in my teaching of poems, takes place in that process we call revision. Often revision means no more than aesthetic consistency—we try to make all the parts of our poems line up and be equally well-written. But there's another form of revision that asks us to revise ourselves, to address those parts of the poem where we have skipped over the hard facts of existence or, on the other hand, saw only the despair of living but not the joy.

I know my teaching of writing works well only when I can help the student see himself or herself more clearly. I now spend a lot of time with my students just talking—about their lives, their families, their hopes and agonies. I try to bring the honesty of those talks into their poems. When I first started writing I looked to see what I cut away. These days I look for those places where I need to expand. And though our age has come to distrust terms like the Muse, there is a voice not my own that I'm learning to listen for.

Let me end with another passage from Adam Zagajewski's book, *Another Beauty*, that could equally well apply to a lifetime of reading as it could to a lifetime: "To wake and fall asleep, drowse off and waken, to pass through seasons of doubt, melancholy dark as lead, indifference, boredom, and then the spells of vitality, clarity, hard and happy work, contentment, gaiety, to remember and forget and recollect again, that an eternal fire burns inside us, a God with an unknown name, whom we will never reach."

two

On Poetry and Reading the Bible

The Art of Devotion
Poetry and Prayer

Attention, taken to its highest degree, is the same thing as prayer. It presupposes faith and love.

—Simone Weil, *Gravity and Grace*

IN HIS ESSAY, "THE SOCIAL Function of Poetry," T. S. Eliot notes that we should distrust those people, especially poets, who talk about what they think poetry ought to do. As Eliot rightly knew, when poets tell us what poetry ought to do, they usually have in mind "the particular kind of poetry they would like to write." I ask you to keep Eliot's warning in mind as I write about so presumptuous a topic as poetry and prayer in an inevitably personal way and with the kind of poetry I would like to write behind my every word.

When I was in graduate school, the poet I felt closest to was George Herbert, the seventeenth-century Anglican priest, and poet of one volume of posthumously published verse, *The Temple*. *The Temple* is comprised of poems that move between the spiritual conflicts of the poet-priest-speaker and the architecture, furnishings, and rituals of the church building in which his daily life is lived. Prayer—which Herbert called "the soul in paraphrase," the "Christian plummet sounding heav'n and earth" ("Prayer 1")—and poetry were daily activities and Herbert, perhaps better than any other writer, knew the tensions between poetry and prayer and the all too often painful and uncrossable distance between the two. But he also knew how poems are a form of prayer, an act of attention in which the poet attends both to God and to what is before him. Herbert knew, as the minister in Marilynne Robinson's *Gilead* knows, that "right worship is right perception."

George Herbert *is* a Christian poet. But Herbert's poetry is not just valuable to those who share his religious beliefs. The poems are not limited to a set of prescribed Christian tenets, and they do not depend on the reader's assent to any specific religious premises. And I hope, too, that the framework of my experience as a Christian does not limit my remarks, though that tradition is clearly the one I know and from which I am speaking.

As in all good religious poetry, Herbert's *Temple* records the search for a life of the spirit. For those to whom religion means comfort and peace of mind, Herbert brings the agonizing appraisal of the often-duplicitous workings of his own mind and heart. To those who would believe in an easy faith, Herbert reminds us that God must be *experienced,* and that such an experience necessarily involves the difficulty of distinguishing "between what one really feels and what one would like to feel," as T. S. Eliot nicely put it, singling out Herbert for his fidelity to the truth.

What I admire in Herbert's poems is their resolute desire to plumb the reality of their spiritual concerns. My own work aims at and usually falls short of what I find in Herbert: poems that are always in the process of self-scrutiny and testing, always in search of truths to live by. Herbert's poems continually question what he feels and thinks, what is illusory and what is not, and how he should best live his life. The essential task of his poems is to articulate, as faithfully as Herbert can, the experienced reality of the cosmos as a creation, an ordered, meaningful work of the Creator. Of course what is meant by "ordered" and "meaningful" has been called continually into question in the intervening years between the seventeenth century and our own time.

That acknowledgment brings me to the second writer who lies behind this piece and my poems: Simone Weil, the French theologian and philosopher. In her essay, "Attention and Will," Weil draws a distinction between these two things. Attention is a form of waiting, as is prayer. It is the opposite of will, where the will tries to understand the world by appropriating the world to its understanding. For Weil, the world we live in is a mystery and in order to feel comfortable in such a world, human beings often end up by loving what is imaginary—our own dreams and self-deceptions. We try to squeeze that mystery into theories and explanations, instead of suffering the "contradictions" (why, for instance, the truly innocent suffer so much more than anyone could ever deserve) that the mind comes up against in the very depths of our being. The title of my book, *Against Consolation,* comes from Weil's notion that "we must not weep so we that we may not be comforted." We comfort ourselves, that is, when we erase the contradictions of living rather than suffering them.

Weil insists that to live honestly in the world we must learn to wait. Waiting teaches us three important things: first, the deepest order is not within our ability or art's ability to create. Instead, it is something that finds us. We are able to experience its various manifestations—truth, beauty, goodness, God—both within and outside ourselves, but only if we are open enough, vulnerable enough, unprejudiced and attentive enough. Second, we must suffer the gap between the profound goodness of being and the painful, imperfect world human beings continue to create. As Wallace Stevens put it, we are an "unhappy people in a happy world." Third, we must love this world—not to figure it out or even understand it, but as Wendell Berry says, "to suffer and rejoice in it as it is." Weil's metaphor of waiting is a crucial one for our time. What Weil meant by waiting and what I mean by waiting is, perhaps, best expressed by T. S. Eliot in his *Four Quartets:*

> I said to my soul be still and wait without hope
> For hope would be hope of the wrong thing;
> wait without love
> For love would be love of the wrong thing;
> there is yet faith
> But the faith and the love and the hope are all
> in the waiting.

Waiting admits the profound limits of the ego and the need for an openness to that which lies outside the ego. It is a form of attention, and as Weil says, "attention is, in its highest degree, the same thing as prayer."

Let me turn to prayer (and by prayer I mean monastic prayer) for a moment and then back to what I see as some of the commonalities between poetry and prayer. The essential simplicity of monastic prayer, what's often called the "prayer of the heart," consists, Thomas Merton writes in his book, *Contemplative Prayer,* of "interior recollection, the abandonment of distracting thoughts and the humble invocation of the Lord Jesus with words from the Bible in a spirit of intense faith." Such prayer is a way of keeping oneself in the presence of God, and of bringing oneself face to face with that falsity of the self that seeks to live for itself alone. As Merton says, by "prayer of the heart" we seek God himself present in the depths of our being and meet him there by invoking the name of Jesus in faith, wonder, and love." In this sense, all acts of prayer might be seen as preparations and purifications to ready oneself for what Merton called a "confrontation with the Abyss," the dread of standing naked and defenseless before God. To stand there is to "stand in our nothingness without explanation, without theories, completely dependent upon [God] for his providential care, and in dire need of his grace, his mercy, his light of faith."

For Merton, prayer is necessary because "the mystery of God, of the divine redemption and of his infinite mercy is generally nebulous and unreal even to 'men of faith.' We unconsciously distort true perspectives, falsify the real, and lack the courage to respond to it." To place Merton in the language of Simone Weil we might say that to stand in the Abyss, one must assume a posture of waiting. Art, prayer, faith: all three require openness to mystery and an acute awareness of the human desire to escape that mystery.

The poet John Keats said that a poet must be capable of Negative Capability, "of being in uncertainties, mysteries, doubts, without any irritable reaching after fact and conclusion." And Simone Weil insists that "extreme attention is what constitutes the creative faculty in man and the only extreme attention is religious." For her, "the amount of creative genius in any period is strictly in proportion to the amount of extreme attention and thus of authentic religion in that period."

I do not mean to conflate poetry and prayer. If poetry and prayer have this quality of attention in common, poetry rarely if ever achieves the condition of prayer. As Weil says, only "absolutely unmixed attention is prayer." George Herbert, as I've said, knew the tensions between poetry and prayer. One of the first poems the reader encounters in *The Temple* is a poem in the shape of an altar. It begins:

> A broken ALTAR, Lord, thy servant rears,
> Made of a heart, and cemented with tears
> Whose parts are as thy hand did frame;
> No workman's tool hath touch'd the same.

Herbert is well aware here of the biblical injunction in Exodus 20:25, "And if thou wilt make me an altar of stone, thou shall not build it of hewn stone: for if thou lift up thy tool upon it, thou hast polluted it." Herbert claims straight-away not to have made the altar, but simply to have gathered the necessary parts (his heart and tears) so that God might "frame" them into an altar.

And yet the first thing the poem does—even before its words are read—is call attention to its visual shape, to the skill of the poet who, presumably, arranged the poem as the ingenious visual altar we see on the page. And if, in the course of the poem, Herbert helps the reader discover, just as he discovered, that even the very shapeliness of the poem belongs to God and not the self, the question the poem raises is a difficult one to put to rest: where does the poet disappear and God appear? If the question is phrased in terms of prayer and poetry, we might ask, How can a poem, which is, as the Greek word *poesis* implies, a making, an arrangement and form, ever be entirely free of the "I" which made it, which shaped it into a form? The short answer is: it cannot.

Herbert's poems often focus the reader on this very paradox. Herbert wants to write well-crafted poems and he wants those poems to praise God. But he readily admits that the very language and forms that he employs as a poet can only "say amiss / This or that is." Still, it is precisely this acknowledgment that is one of the deepest connections between poetry and prayer. As Eliot says, each poetic "venture" is "a wholly new beginning / a raid on the inarticulate." That is, both poetry and prayer acknowledge the limits of the ego. In this sense, their origins are rooted in invocation—a calling out to or an invoking of that which cannot be seen or logically understood and which, ultimately, cannot be put into language. As Richard Wilbur writes in his poem "For Dudley," "All that we do / Is touched with ocean, yet we remain / On the shore of what we know."

For me, prayer and, as Eliot puts it, the "particular kind of poetry" I admire and "would like to write," reside at this shoreline boundary of the inarticulate. Both prayer and poetry embody a longing and a reaching toward the inconceivable. And both refuse to be silent when they face that mystery, though they both admit that all words reach towards and end up in silence.

The "particular kind of poetry" I am speaking of finds its modern ancestry in Rilke, in Wallace Stevens and T. S. Eliot, and its more contemporary expression in the work of writers such as Charles Wright, Richard Wilbur, and Czeslaw Milosz. The poetics I'm talking about honors what Heidegger called the "unfolding of unconcealedness." Here is Rilke, in his eighth Duino Elegy, in a translation by Galway Kinnell:

> And we: spectators, always, everywhere,
> Turned toward all this and never beyond it.
> It overfills us. We arrange it. It falls apart.
> We arrange it again, and fall apart ourselves.

In his very fine essay, "Raiding the Inarticulate: Mysticism, Poetics, and the Unlanguageable," Mark Burrows says about these lines from Rilke that "attentiveness to the visible calls us not to look *for* something, but to dwell *in* this world by letting it be *as it is,* by learning to see it in its essential dynamism and to know ourselves as held within the widest orbits—and yet as never contained by it since 'it falls apart' as we also do."

Poetry and prayer are ways of keeping myself present to both the presence and absence of God and attentive to the reality of the world as it is. Thus far I've talked about the first half of the Weil's epigraph to this piece—"Attention, taken to its highest degree, is the same thing as prayer." Now I want to talk about the second half of Weil's statement: "It (attention taken to its highest degree) presupposes faith and love."

Let me illustrate what I mean by turning to my favorite novel. The character of Lily Briscoe in Virginia Woolf's *To the Lighthouse* paints two pictures during the course of the novel. The first painting—all angles and blocks of colors—attempts to symbolize the relationship between the still living Mrs. Ramsay and her husband. Lily keeps repeating to herself "this is what I see, this is what I see" as she tries to command her painting into being. That painting—is, importantly, a failure. Lily arranges, but the painting has no life at its center. Lily's art keeps trying to rationally understand Mr. and Mrs. Ramsay, seeing each of them and their relationship in various and always limiting unities.

In the novel's last section, Lily begins the painting—years later—once again, starting afresh. Mrs. Ramsay has died, there has been a World War, and the summer house where everyone gathers has nearly gone to ruin before being brought back to life. Lily is on the shore, painting, but mostly remembering all that has passed as she watches Mr. Ramsay, Cam, and James sail to the lighthouse—a journey which itself was planned but never undertaken those many years ago when Lily was working at her first painting. Now as Lily remembers, searching, as Woolf puts it, "among the infinite series of impressions time has laid down," she begins her painting. But once again the painting resists her.

Woolf suggests that this resistance has much to do with the detached way Lily remembers; Lily, a single woman who pursues a serious career, has always resented Mrs. Ramsay's domestic arrangements and envied her domestic happiness. Now, Lily remembers the past with the sense almost of triumph as she thinks of all that has changed despite Mrs. Ramsay's attempts during her life to arrange things.

But as memories make present all that is absent and, as Lily suffers the past into life, admitting to herself that she, too, cannot control a world where there is no "safety," where everything is "startling, unexpected, unknown" and yet "all was miracle," she finally cries out, *Mrs. Ramsay! Mrs. Ramsay!*—it is this moment of utterly painful emotion, of simply loving the dead Mrs. Ramsay in all her contradictoriness, which becomes the true center of her painting. *Art cannot redeem what it does not love*—a motto Ellen Bryant Voigt claims to have tacked up to her study door in one of her poems—lies at the heart of Woolf's understanding. Lily redeems the lost years only when she loves that which is outside herself—the particularity and otherness of the Ramseys. We could say that she comes to truly know herself and her art only in attending to and ultimately loving the irreducible otherness of Mrs. Ramsay. Attention can only truly come with love, since only love lets the world be as it is.

In a little book I found recently on a bench (among other books with a sign that said Free Books) where I work, I found this passage: "in that public and sacramental gathering of the Church we call Liturgy we are present at a revelation of God . . . uttering His powerful and life-giving Word." The book is called *Reflections on the Jesus Prayer*, and the author is identified only as a priest in the Byzantine Church. The book is a phrase-by-phrase dwelling on the Jesus Prayer in an attempt to teach this basic precept: "prayer is nothing else but attentiveness to God's presence."

In churches, liturgies give a voice to biblical memories; in monasteries, monks chant the cycles of the Psalms; in individual prayer we hope to attend to God's presence; and what we listen for in the "sound of words," Wallace Stevens tells us, is a "finality, a perfection, an unalterable vibration" that brings us closer (since metaphor always seeks to bring the world closer in its act of finding correspondences) to the "muddy center," the first idea, God.

Poetry reminds us that we are, to use Wallace Stevens's words again, "thinkers without final thoughts / In an always incipient cosmos." And poetry and prayer both remind us that we reside at the boundary of the inarticulate. At that boundary we attend, waiting as Czeslaw Milosz says in "Against Incomprehensible Poetry," for the "veil of everyday habit [to fall] away [so that] what we paid no attention, because it struck us as so ordinary, [might be] revealed as miraculous."

I want to end with a little story. In 1938, with Europe well on its way towards the horrors of World War II, Simone Weil spent ten days, from Palm Sunday to Easter Sunday, at a monastery in northwest France. Biographers of Weil mark those ten days as an important turning-point in her spiritual development. While at the monastery, Weil took to reciting the poem "Love 3" by George Herbert again and again as an aid to meditation. She wrote later that as she recited the poem, she felt "a presence more personal, more certain, and more real than that of a human being; it was inaccessible both to sense and to imagination, and it resembled the love that irradiates the tenderest smile of somebody who loves." The experience was a kind of conversion, "the thought of the passion of Christ," as Weil puts it in *Waiting for God,* "enter[ing] into my being once and for all."

Consider this: Weil's experience of the love of Christ occurs as she recites a poem that she uses as a prayer; the poem she prayed, "Love 3," was written by the poet, George Herbert, a seventeenth-century Anglican priest who wanted, more than all else, for his poems to become prayers, for the bits and pieces of biblical verses he often inserted in his poems to suffice both as poetry and as sufficient praise of God. And for a moment in that French monastery, poem and prayer were, as they were perhaps in their origin, one and the same.

Something More

IN HIS REVIEW OF *THE LITERARY Guide to the Bible* for the *New Yorker*, George Steiner warned against the separation "made in the name of current rationalism and agnosticism" between a "theological religious experiencing of biblical texts and a literary one." Steiner argued instead for writing which would help us "to understand in what ways the Bible and the demands of answerability it puts upon us" are unlike other literary texts. Northrop Frye's *The Great Code* and the two books that followed, *Words with Power* and *The Double Vision,* all address the complicated problems of "answerability" that the Bible presents to its readers. Although Frye explicitly states that his approach to the Bible is that of a literary critic, and although these works certainly provide a critical apparatus for recognizing relationships between Western literary texts and the Bible, Frye's task from the outset has been to establish how the Bible is "more" than a work of literature, "whatever more means."

For Frye, the way in which the Bible is more than a work of literature begins with his concept—certainly not new with him as Frye acknowledges—of "metaphorical literalism." Frye understands the paradoxical nature of his claim. While the narrative the Bible tells, stretching from creation to apocalypse, is literal and true, the true literal meaning is imaginative and poetic. Frye is quick to point out the usual fallacy of what is meant by literally true, namely, what is "descriptively accurate." Literalism of this kind is what Paul calls the letter that kills. Such literalism is simply false and connected, for Frye, to the worst elements of organized religions—bigotry, cruelty, intolerance, hatred.

While not denying the historicity of biblical events and persons, what Frye calls for, then, is an "imaginative literalism" that recognizes the "literal basis of faith in Christianity is a mythical and metaphorical basis, not one founded on historical facts or logical propositions." For

Frye, myth and metaphor are a "primitive form of awareness, established long before the distinction of subject and object became normal."

Just as myth is neither historical nor anti-historical, but counter-historical, metaphor is neither logical nor illogical, but counter-logical. As such, the question we should bring to biblical stories is not the objective—did the events happen just as we are told?—but rather: how do we stand with respect to the events' revelation of God? If we approach the Bible solely as literary critics, then its stories, no matter how beautifully wrought in terms of their imaginative vision and formal properties, are "simply stories, considered with the suspended judgment of the imagination without relation to the area we vaguely describe as *truth*." Thus beyond the usual metaphorical-literal level where stories are only stories, there is for Frye the "polysemous" nature of the Bible in which the unity of the biblical stories form a myth to live by, "transformed from the kind of story we can construct ourselves to a spiritual story of what has created and continues to re-create us."

I want to read Frye's ideas of metaphorical literalism in the context of Gerald Brun's book *Hermeneutics Ancient and Modern*, specifically his chapter on Luther. As Luther put it, he did not wish to understand Scripture by his spirit or others' but solely by *its* spirit. Scripture, then, is not "so much an object of understanding as a component of it; what one understands when one understands the scriptural texts is not anything conceptual and extractable as a meaning."

What does one understand?—the life of faith which seeks understanding as informed by the Scriptures. As in Augustine, one must already have understood a text (in the sense of that which it teaches) to be able to interpret its language. As Bruns formulates it, the hermeneutical situation which Luther describes is one in which "the reader is not so much the interpreter as the interpreted." This is Luther's great reform: to encounter the Bible in the spirit in which it was written, an encounter which is not concerned with deciphering a text's meanings but with "the event of the interpretation itself." Scripture must be experienced. The reader cannot be a "disengaged rational subject" (Bruns). As opposed to the idea of a text as a purely analytical object on which interpretation is done, Luther posits a text that inscribes itself in the reader.

In Frye, too, the text is something that confronts the reader: "sooner or later we have to study . . . our own experience in reading it"; the reader in Frye is *exposed* to the Bible, made vulnerable by a God who "drowns the world in a fit of anger and re-peoples in a fit of remorse," a trickster God who calls all our human formulations into question. Frye's "double vision" entails both a growing insight into our conditioned limits and the growing ability (as we are transformed by the biblical myth) to separate our human mirror of God from God's reality.

Frye's "double vision" requires, as it did for Luther, the rehabilitation of Scripture as a "pneumatic text" in which the meaning of a word "is its force" (Bruns). While the Bible is written in the language of literature, in the language of myth and metaphor, its language, according to Frye, is intended to convey a vision of spiritual life; its "metaphors become, as purely literary metaphors cannot, metaphors to live in." As Gabriel Josipovici puts it in his *The Book of God*, the Bible wants to "draw me out of myself." Understandably, then, Frye's great hope in both *The Great Code* and *Words with Power* is that we have come to a new phase in our understanding of language and, subsequently, are in a position to restore some of the original resources of language in which words were "words with power."

More than anything else, Frye seeks to understand the linguistic idiom of the Bible, a form of expression for which he adopts the term *kerygma*. *Kerygma* is a mode of rhetoric that must be seen, Frye says, from "both of its two aspects—metaphor and concern." "Concern" is best explained by Frye: "in concerned address a much more comprehensive response from all aspects of the personality is called for." Though it would have been helpful if Frye had written more specifically about his understanding of *kerygma*, what Bruns says about Luther's hermeneutics might be applied here: it "presupposes a relationship to the Scripture that is not a grammarian's relationship to a textual object but that of a listener to a voice" (Bruns).

To restore our sense of "words with power," requires an experiencing of metaphor and myth that is not an intellectual hunt for archetypes and typologies (though Frye's charts may sometimes make it feel this way), but rather a radically metaphorical disclosure of the "truth" of the biblical narrative.

To help with this restoration, Frye, employing a schema from Vico's *New Science,* divides the history of Western *language* into three phases: the first phase is poetic or metaphorical discourse in which the later distinction between figured and literal language hardly exists; the second phase (from around the time of Plato) is called the metyonymic phase by Frye and in this phase words become the outward expression of inner thoughts, and metaphorical discourse becomes subordinate to the truth of metyonymic or conceptual discourse; the third phase dates from the sixteenth century; in this phase both metaphorical and metyonymic language are subject to the truth of language which is primarily descriptive of an objective natural order.

Frye lays out this schema for two reasons: our understanding of the Bible today depends in part on understanding how the Bible has been interpreted within a tradition in which the criteria for truthfulness has privileged discursive discourse over metaphorical discourse. The result is that we are left with myths that have become purely literary. Though Frye admits that much of the Bible is "contemporary with the second-phase separation of the dialectical from the poetic," he argues that the Bible's origins lie in the first metaphorical phase. Biblical language never falls "wholly into the conventions of the second phase" because there are "no true rational arguments in the Bible." For Frye, biblical Hebrew is an "obsessively concrete language" that eschews abstraction; and the New Testament, despite its late date, shares this attitude toward language. Such concreteness is a trait, Frye argues, that belongs to the metaphorical phase of language. Once we recognize the Bible's essentially metaphorical language despite the "domination" of the later phases, we can begin the arduous task of finding our way back to a God who "may not be so much dead as entombed in a dead language." Thus Frye's task in *The Great Code* and *Words with Power* is to restore the mythical and metaphorical basis of the Bible (and in so doing restore, paradoxically, the literal basis of faith).

It might help here to talk for a moment about how Robert Alter's books, especially *The World of Biblical Literature*, are interested in the same question as Frye—how is the Bible a unique work of literature? And, it might help to talk about where these two divide. Alter and Frye agree that historical criticism of the Bible is rooted "in a view of truth associated with nineteenth century positivism that does not sit well with any sense of the moral or spiritual authority of Scripture." Alter and Frye, that is, both share the same interest in closing the distance between reader and text that I spoke about earlier. And Alter's interest in bringing the tools of literary analysis to bear on the Bible, like Frye's, are in the service of "opening ourselves to something that deserves to be called their authority, whether we attribute that authority solely to the power of the human imagination *or* to a transcendent source of illumination that kindled the imagination of the writers to express itself through . . . particular literary means" (emphasis mine).

But here is also the place where the two part company. Alter, who, perhaps, more than any recent writer on the Bible has taught us how to attend to the poetic and narrative properties of the Bible, is not only content with that "or" but is highly suspicious of anyone who would push for "more." As Alter concludes: "the covenantal urgency of the Biblical writers impelled them on a bold and finally impossible project: they sought to use literature to go irrevocably beyond itself. . . ." We might say that, in the end, Alter is comfortable with interpretation that attends with acumen and a generous spirit to the infinite particularities of the Bible's poetic and narrative authority.

Frye, on the other hand, wants to attend to the "event of the interpretation itself." As Bruns says about Luther's hermeneutics: "interpretation is an event that moves in two directions. It is not possible to interpret a text without being interpreted by it in turn." In the context of explaining why we cannot talk about the Bible in simple either/or terms (history or fiction), Frye notes that myth is neither history nor fiction; mythic knowledge is always a matter of recognition—a myth's proclamation, as Frye says, is not "so much this is true as this is what you must know." Myths are stories that "tell a society what is important for it to know." Myth's haunting power for Frye is linked to the way it is not a literal explanation of something in the world, but an expression of the primitive, in the sense that the primitive expresses a "fundamental and persisting link with reality."

Frye situates both his Viconian schema and his discussion of myth and metaphor beside the debate between Peacock and Shelley. Frye agrees with Shelley's claim that "'progress' is always a progress toward disaster" since such progress ignores what poets have always known: "every mind is a primitive mind." The Viconian schema of the metaphorical-metonymic-descriptive sequence is provided for us so that we recognize that such a sequence is not progress, but rather a means of occluding the very nature of metaphor and myth, of poetry and the arts of which mythology is a part.

As Frye points out, "literature always assumes, in its metaphors, a relation between human consciousness and its natural environment that passes beyond—in fact, outrages and violates—the ordinary common sense based on a permanent separation of subject and object." Frye directs us toward great gift of metaphor: to "defamiliarize" so that the world can be seen again in its uniqueness. Frye notes the creative and imaginative quality of myth because he sees a link between myth and the primary function of literature: "to keep re-creating the first or metaphorical phase of language." In Frye, literary history is the constant attempt on the part of poets to restore our original relationship to what Wallace Stevens called the "muddy center." As Frye understands, the poet's task is always, as Eliot said, to purify the language of the tribe so that we might see what kind of world we are really in, so that we might have, as Stevens said, the "intensest rendezvous with the world."

Myths are autonomous, then, because they are creative and imaginative, because their truth is inside their verbal structure, not outside it. But this is only half the picture, as Frye well knows. Just as the oratorical style of the Bible united the poetic and the concerned for Frye, myth unites its poetic aspect as a story with its social function. In both its poetic and social aspects, myth is a "program of action for a specific society."

More importantly for Frye, in both these aspects myth "relates not to the actual but to the possible." Here's Frye: "The general principle involved here (the kernel of actual history in biblical stories) is that if anything historically true is in the Bible, it is there not because it is historically true but for different reasons. The reasons have presumably to do with spiritual profundity or significance."

Frye's point is simply that proving the historicity of biblical passages is a fruitless enterprise when weighed against their significance as stories that teach us more about the "possible" than the actual. Myth and the mythic mode of the Bible are crucial because they keep confronting us with fundamental realities that are not of our own making. To move towards the "possible" involves, as Frye says, seeing "an element of illusion in what is really there, and something real in fantasies about what might be there instead." It is here that the imaginative and the concerned "begin to unite."

Metaphor for Frye is the vehicle for those dual aspects—the poetic and the concerned—of myth. For Frye, remember, the letter of the biblical text is radically metaphorical. But when Frye argues that the Bible's origins are connected to the metaphorical phase of language, he is not talking about the use of metaphors (of figuration that embellish a narrative), but rather pointing toward the Bible's "mode of symbolization." (A phrase of my colleague's James Kee). It is not important, say, that the David and Bathsheba story contains very little figuration; what is important is the way even the historically rooted David story is itself radically metaphorical in its complex articulation. "Radically" because the story is not simply a part of some self-reflective system of interlocking archetypes, but rather a story that contains the power to interpret us, to make us see past our own conditioned limits and help us towards a truer understanding of the mysteries of our living and dying. What is important is the way David's and our self-identity is interrupted by the unfolding of the story's events.

This effort is connected, as I mentioned earlier, to Frye's "double vision" which entails the recognition of our own "conditioned limits" and a separating of our human mirror of God from God's reality. The process of separation is connected to the way these paradigmatic Bible stories exhibit the three levels Frye spoke of in connection with Milton's *Paradise Regained*: demonic parody, redemptive power, and apocalyptic vision. The demonic level is connected to our imprisonment in what Frye calls our single vision, which "sees in him [God] the reflection of human panic and rage, its love of cruelty and domination, and, when it accepts such a God, calls on him to justify the maintaining of these things in human life."

Such a demonic state of being is always connected to a lack of awareness of our own "conditioned limits." We see, as Job first saw, a God who should be acting (we think), but is not, according to human standards of justice. That God of course is what Frye calls the "human mirror." The redemptive level cannot begin until we allow ourselves to be questioned, until we run up against what cannot be explained by any human formulation.

As Simone Weil understands, the "contradictions the mind comes up against—these are the only realities: they are the criterion of the real." When contradictions are experienced at the very depths of our being, according to Weil, "it is the cross." The cross, where the dying of our human understanding of God takes place, is the threshold of the apocalyptic state or what Frye sometimes calls the "ecstatic" state and is linked to his "double vision" in which we recognize at last, as Job recognized, we have taken the "face of God in vain."

Michael Dolzani, in his essay, "The Ashes of the Stars: Northrop Frye and the Trickster God," writes that Frye "began his career identifying with the Romantic revolutionary solution of Blake, who rejected the negative trickster-God as a symbol of false authority, and found the true trickster deity in the creative spirit of humanity." But Dolzani posits a different late Frye, one who "supplements such a solution with the vision of a positive trickster-God as a mysterious Other who may liberate us by breaking through the egocentric limitations of our own ambitions and desires." It is this Other that breaks though our "egocentric limitations" that I was hoping to catch in my placement of Frye alongside Weil rather than Blake.

Metaphor and mythical language are at the heart of Frye's reading of the Bible because they are the only mode of language that says "both 'is' and 'is not'" simultaneously. Unity in Frye is never synonymous with uniformity as Frye points out in his discussion of a God who is "irascible and whimsical," the trickster-God of Frye:

> What, for example, are we to do with a God who drowns the world in a fit of anger and repeoples it in a fit of remorse, promising never to do it again; a god who curses the ground Adam is forced to cultivate after his fall, but removes the curse after Noah makes a tremendous holocaust of animals. . . .

As Dolzani nicely puts it: "if you have such a God on your hands, you are going to have to struggle." The struggle in Frye, as Dolzani understands, is "with the Word in an attempt to recreate both its aspects: as text and as vision of God."

Such a struggle involves what Heidegger called "undergoing an experience of language." Here is Heidegger in his essay "The Nature of Language": "To undergo an experience with something—be it a thing, a person, or a god—means that this something befalls us, strikes us, comes over us and transforms us . . . the experience is not of our own making."

The Bible, for Frye, is kergymatic because rather than persuade, it proclaims, taking "one out of oneself." Frye goes on to note that such an "utterance" is "one charged with such intensity, urgency, or authority that it penetrates the defenses of the human receiving apparatus and creates a new channel of response."

As I tried to lay out in my turning to Bruns and Luther, the reading experience for Frye contains an experience of divestiture. We must be divested of all our familiar human concepts which we rely on to make sense of the world. Dolzani quotes this notebook entry of Frye: "All reading begins in the revolt against narcissism: when a book stops reflecting your own prejudices, whether for or against what you 'see in it' & begins to say something closer to what it does say, the core of the reality in the 'objective' aspect of it takes shape and you are wrestling with an angel."

At the heart of Dolzani's insight into Frye is the interrelationship between the way of vacancy ("the *katabasis* or descent into the 'nothing'"), the "negation of a negation," and the possible transformation that may take place with the vision of a mysterious Other who breaks through our egocentric limitations. The descent is into the dark side of the divine nature which we are forced to confront (if we can bear it) in the realities of loss that collapse all our illusions of presence. As Dolzani puts it in a beautifully worded paragraph: "He [God] takes away paradise from Adam and Eve; everything from Job; himself from Jesus . . .; Beatrice from Dante; Regina Olsen from Kierkegaard; the entire past from Marcel Proust; Helen Frye from her husband."

This descent may lead to the "negation of a negation." Though we must be divested of our "conditioned limits" in the descent, divested of the mirror of God we create out of our needs and desires through a process of loss that leaves us exposed and vulnerable, this divestiture also makes it possible for the reader to be transformed. It makes possible the "negation of a negation," which involves both a struggle against what Frye calls an "otherness, what the imagination is not" and an act of faith in the "creative process itself." Such a struggle makes possible what Wallace Stevens called "a revelation in words by means of words."

Only in that emptied condition of being can the Spirit be experienced (as in Luther's hermeneutics). The ego, which cannot escape the world of subject and object, must be descended into. It must be experienced for what it produces: the darkness of corruption. The contrary to the ego is Spirit which Dolzani defines this way: "not just human natural energy, Freud's libido, Blake's Orc, but rather the indwelling of the Holy Spirit, our deepest identity which is nevertheless also our identity with the divine." Spirit, as Frye tells us, is "identified in the New Testament both with God and with the kind of understanding response it wants us to develop about God." Spirit, in the sense of this "understanding response," is characterized by an intimacy in which understanding takes place, an intimacy whereby one's self-identity is interrupted by the other (as Levinas speaks of).

To summarize: first, a trickster-God is necessary because such a God, everywhere apparent in the Bible, crosses our own willful paths with a reality not of our making. Only such a God can explode the "impasses of our own contradictory and impossible desires."

Secondly, as Frye notes in *Words with Power*, to arrive at any kind of verbal understanding of the Bible we have to "go through the territory of literature." The territory of literature, of course, is myth and metaphor, and the counter-historical and counter-logical worlds they open. As Dolzani puts it, it is "indeed a question of metaphors, and a great visionary is God's fool or juggler judged according to how many metaphors he can keep in the air at the same time, each of them a supplement and counterbalance to the others."

Thirdly, while the imaginative world of literature offers us a model of the essential freedom that is needed if the reader is to interpret and be interpreted by the text, the Bible is also a different kind of text: it is uniquely kerygmatic for Frye because it offers a myth to live by, a means of "reordering the direction of one's life." If we "go through" the territory of literature, we also have to go "out of it on our way to something else." The "something else" is the genuinely kerygmatic which, Frye tells us, is the point at which "subject and object merge in an immediate verbal world, where a Word not our own, though also our own, proclaims and a Spirit not our own, though also our own, responds."

At the end of *Words with Power*, Northrop Frye returns to the paradigmatic tale of Job. Job cannot see at first what kind of trial he is undergoing once everything is taken from him. Though Job mistakenly thinks his trial is one of accusation and judgment, his trial, Frye explains, is really one which is purgatorial, "a testing and refining operation" directed toward "what one can still be." Our position as readers in relation to the Bible is also a purgatorial trial for Frye. The God we encounter there is, as in Job, beyond all else, utterly baffling, utterly outside our human ideas of what God should be. And so it must be. Explaining the phrase, "he that hath ears to hear, let him hear," Frye notes that it is "not an elitism restricting the message only to those previously chosen to hear it," but rather "an appeal to make one's response depend as little as possible on the conventions of one's conditioning and prejudices."

Only with such "an understanding response" can the Bible begin to interpret us. When God speaks from the whirlwind, then, it is not to answer Job's why but to direct him toward what he "can still be." Of course, no objective answer could ever suffice: "the mysteries represented in metaphor by the first creation in Genesis, the mysteries of birth and death and 'thrownness' can never be understood because they can never be objectified." And Job has to become an entirely different person—one who realizes that his question, why is this happening to me?, is entirely irrelevant.

As Frye knows, Job has to become a "participant" in the initial creation that God represents to him. As we must. To Frye, the Bible's mode of discourse creates such encounters. The force of its words exhorts us to "be / In the difficulty of what it is to be" (Stevens). More than anything else, Northrop Frye's last three books try to clear a space in which we can experience the "double vision" for which the Bible prepares us: the recognition of our own limits of understanding; and, after that, "perhaps the terrifying and welcome voice" that "annihilate[s] everything we thought we knew, and restore[s] everything we never lost."

Metaphors To Live In

IWAS RAISED A MISSOURI Synod Lutheran. What does that mean? Luther might have questioned. In part, it meant two years of Luther's Catechism and Bible study in eighth and ninth grades, a public examination in front of Grace Evangelical's mostly German immigrant congregation, and finally confirmation and first communion. For me personally it meant a growing love of the Bible and the mysteries of interpretation. And metaphor. In my first year of catechism class I asked the minister if he believed Moses's staff actually turned into a serpent. Of course, I didn't know then what exactly I was asking, or even what answer I wanted to hear. An adolescent wise guy, I asked my question more to entrap the minister than for the actual answer. His answer—an unequivocal yes—stunned me. In retrospect, I see that moment as the unofficial start of my long journey with the Bible, metaphor, and poetry.

Skip ahead fifty or so years, and here I am still thinking about the Bible—specifically about how the Bible is "more" than a work of literature. In the last essay, I sketched out what I learned from Northrop Frye about reading the Bible. For the last twenty years or so of my teaching English at the College of the Holy Cross, I taught a course called "The Bible and Literature." Note that "and"—not the Bible *as* Literature but The Bible *and* Literature. The course was indebted to my reading of Northrop Frye's three books on the Bible: *The Great Code* (its subtitle, *The Bible and Literature*, gave my course its title), *Words with Power*, and *The Double Vision*. As I explained in the last essay, Frye, in his book *The Double Vision,* coins the phrase "metaphorical literalism" for the Bible's mode of language. While not denying the historicity of biblical events and persons, Frye suggests what we should bring to biblical stories is not the objective—did the events happen just as we are told?—but rather: how do we stand with respect to the events' revelation of God?

For Frye, too, the text is something that confronts the reader: "sooner or later we have to study. . .our own experience in reading it"; the reader for Frye is *exposed* to the Bible, made vulnerable by a God who "drowns the world in a fit of anger and re-peoples it in a fit of re-morse," a trickster God who calls all our human formulations into question. As I've said, Frye's "double vision" entails both a growing insight into the limits of our constructed prejudices and beliefs and the growing ability (as we are transformed by the biblical myth) to separate our human mirror of God from God's reality. While the Bible is written in the language of literature, of myth and metaphor, its language is intended to convey a vision of spiritual life; its "metaphors become, as purely literary metaphors cannot, metaphors to live in."

With Frye's ideas in mind, I'd like to think about the story of Abraham as a metaphor to "live in." And I'd like to think of Abraham as a metaphor for the biblical reader. Like Abraham, we encounter a God who forces us to confront the limits of our rational human understanding. And as a reader we must "live in" Abraham's choices and, in so doing, come to experience what living faithfully might mean.

The outlines of this Genesis story are well known. God's call to Abram comes in the context of a scattered and divided humanity. He has been chosen for God's historical purpose; God will make a nation of a man, Abraham of Abram. The promise: abundant progeny will characterize Abraham's blessing and a displaced humanity will find its new home.

But there is a series of obstacles: Abram and Sarah do not have any children, and Sarah, we're told, is beyond child-bearing age; Abram, while faithful and insightful, also *thinks* he can know what God wants, and often his rationale for this or that action (lying about Sarah in Egypt, sleeping with Hagar) results in precisely the wrong result. And, when Sarah does give birth to Isaac with God's blessing, God asks Abraham to sacrifice this only son who is to become Israel!

I remember playing Bob Dylan's *Highway 61* over and over in college, the lyrics asking what I knew, all too frighteningly, I had to make sense of: "God said to Abraham, 'Kill me a son.' Abe said, 'Man, you must be puttin' me on.' God said, 'No.' Abe say, 'What?'" Yes, *What?*—like Abraham we are confronted by God's request. No story in Genesis is as terrifying, as powerful, as mysterious, and, finally, as elusive.

We might say that Abraham, like Job, like each of us, has to live through his fear of God as totally Other so his love might become the love of God's real presence. The authors of Genesis imagine an Abraham constantly on the move, responding to events, and experiencing the divine as an imperative that breaks down old certainties. He is not allowed to approach his God with any preconceived ideas; in the story, he travels perpetually forward to the perpetually new. And, as he travels, Abraham undergoes a kind of spiritual education that is necessary to the final event—the trip to Moriah and the sacrifice of Isaac.

This trip must be seen in the light of the story's narrative events. It is an event that can only come at the end of this story, for Abram, who, even with his faithful get-up-and-go attitude, would not have been capable of making this trip earlier. Why? Because Abram had not yet learned how to orient himself by God's will rather than his own. The story is a kind of trial-and-error account of a man who learns to move faithfully towards God, learning along the way to eschew what would seem like reasonable solutions to the problems that block God's promised path.

It is a story about seeing. Seeing, which is always a form of understanding in the stories of Genesis, is both positive and negative. On the one hand, seeing can be connected to an intuitive, imaginative understanding that aligns itself with the will of God. We come to see what God shows us. On the other hand, seeing can be an act of our human will to understand what is beyond our understanding. We contract the world to what we can see and understand.

Both these forms of seeing are present in the Abraham story. Abram suffers from his need to understand in human terms what is beyond human understanding. Though God promises to be his shield and make a nation of his seed, Abram postpones and postpones the promise because he often acts out of his own understanding. During the course of his long journey from Abram to Abraham, he must learn that the ultimate sacrifice is his own human understanding, his need to understand a future he has not yet lived and thus cannot know. He must learn, that is, to see what it is that God will show him as time unfolds. What Abram slowly learns is just *how* God provides, which is certainly not in the way he (or we) thought God would or should.

This story is not a test or trial in the sense that God needs Abraham to prove things to him. The question to ask is: What does *Abraham* need to move fully towards God? By the time he sets out to Moriah, he has learned that what is impossible is possible with God and that his own rational approach has often failed miserably (the two Egyptian episodes, the Hagar episode). And he has learned both to question God (the Sodom and Gomorrah episode)—blind obedience is certainly not what God wants—and to welcome God when he appears in his life as three men/ angels looking for shelter and a good meal.

Throughout this story, Abraham has oscillated between living in God's presence and doing what Abraham thought was reasonable, what he thought God would want him to do. The reader, if open to being interpreted by the story, must learn to "live in" Abram's choices and, in so doing, come to experience both how we want God to conform to our needs and understanding and what, on the other hand, living faithfully might mean.

The reader is not told much about Abram's state of mind as he makes his way to Moriah. There is no certainty, as in any religious quest, that things will work out. In fact, from the moment Abram leaves behind all that is familiar at the story's beginning to the sacrifice of Isaac at its end, indeterminacy is the common link between the events of Abraham's life. We, too, as readers, must enter into the reality of the story's metaphor; we must, it seems, enter the realm of death and meaninglessness (at least in human terms) before meaning can be unfolded both for Abraham and for us in the unfolding of time. Perhaps our lives of faith must involve just such an encounter with the death of human meaning because only in that encounter do we come to recognize that trusting in God to provide may mean giving up all sense of human understanding.

On the third day of his journey, we're told Abraham "looked up and saw the place far away" (Genesis 22:4). Though he didn't know where he was going (as in the story's beginning), the place (Mount Moriah) is recognized at once by Abraham. The recognition is something like knowing there is a person behind you, looking at you, before you turn around.

Or, in my business, like recognizing the voice for a poem when words, jotted down in various combinations, suddenly align themselves syntactically on the blank page and I know at once, yes, that's the voice I've been looking for. And, again, though we cannot know the person we will eventually marry, we recognize that person somewhat immediately. All these examples, of course, depend on experience, on making sense of past experiences and using them as a guide, even if that guide can only take us so far.

The next step is into the abyss, into the unknowable—Abraham builds the fire, carries the knife for his son's sacrifice, and when Isaac calls out "Father!" Abraham responds, "Here I am, my son." This phrase, repeated three times, underscores a parallel relationship with God and Abraham and Abraham and Isaac, suggesting that Abraham understands his role as both child of God and father of Isaac in this moment. His role demanded an act of faith in an unseen presence (God), in the impossible promise that a son would be born to Sarah, and finally in the impossible journey that Abraham has taken since he first got up and went as God asked him.

And where has it led?—here to this altar, where Abraham must sacrifice his human understanding and raise the knife aloft. And here—to that angel that cries "Abraham, Abraham!" and to that last "Here I am" by Abraham. Abraham is fully present to the Lord, fully "there" when God "provides" a ram for sacrifice. The Lord provided precisely what Abraham needed—not just the ram, but the sacrifice of his own rational understanding that kept postulating "this is what God wants, this surely is what God wants."

If we consider Abraham as a metaphor for the reader, then we come up against what Frye calls our own "conditioned limits." When I listened to Dylan as a young man, I could not make sense of why a loving God would ask Abraham to kill his son. Which is to say, I saw God according to my own needs and desires, and those needs could not formulate any reason for God's request to Abraham. Years later, as I began to teach the Bible, I realized Frye's trickster God, everywhere apparent in the Bible, was absolutely necessary; he crosses our own willful paths with a reality not of our making. The God we encounter there is, as in the Abraham story, beyond all else, utterly baffling, utterly outside our human ideas of what God should be. And so it must be. Explaining the phrase, "he that hath ears to hear, let him hear," Frye notes that it is "not an elitism restricting the message only to those previously chosen to hear it," but rather "an appeal to make one's response depend as little as possible on the conventions of one's conditioning and prejudices." Only with such "an understanding response" can the Bible begin to interpret us.

While the imaginative world of literature offers us a model of the essential freedom that is needed if the reader is to interpret and be interpreted by the Bible, the Bible is a different kind of text: it offers a myth to live by, a means, as Frye says, of "reordering the direction of one's life." We read the Abraham story as a literary text; but then we have to go further, we have to leave the territory of literature and go, as Frye puts it, "on our way to something else." The "something else" is the genuinely kerygmatic which, Frye tells us, is the point at which "subject and object merge in an immediate verbal world, where a Word not our own, though also our own, proclaims and a Spirit not our own, though also our own, responds."

A Certain Young Man

A certain young man was following him, wearing nothing but a linen cloth. They caught hold of him, but he left the linen cloth and ran off naked.

—Mark 14: 51–52

THIS INCIDENT APPEARS only in the Gospel of Mark. Biblical commentary, focusing on the adjective "certain" has tried to identify the young man—Mark himself? The owner of the olive garden? Simon of Bethany or Lazarus, both of whom lived nearby? I want to leave him "certain" but nameless, running off into the dark. I want to suggest we all know him, this man who, like ourselves, only desires to be a bystander, to watch from the shadows and pass back into the darkness from which he came.

The sequence of events that precedes this passage about the man running off naked into the dark is significant: the Last Supper; Christ's prediction that one of his disciples will betray him and that all of them will become deserters; Christ's seemingly simple request to his disciples to "keep awake" as he goes off to pray, deeply grieved by his knowledge of what is to come; and his repeated discovery (three times) that his disciples have fallen asleep.

I want to focus on three aspects: first, why the disciples cannot stay awake; secondly, what, perhaps, Jesus might mean when he says, "the hour has come" besides the hour of his betrayal; and third, my own imagined scene between Jesus and the unknown man.

"Keep awake" Jesus tells his disciples, though he knows first-hand (he's been praying that the cup might be taken from him) that the "spirit is willing, but the flesh is weak." The disciples cannot understand the depth of the temptation that lies before them: the temptation here is the human desire to sleep, to remain in the dark when we are confronted by what we do not want to see, either about ourselves or others or the world.

Throughout the Bible, the call is to wake up—to a world that is, but need not be; to a world that is created and, as such, is "Good" (as Genesis 1 uses that word); to the obligations of human freedom and what it means to be created in the "image of God"; to the difficulties of what will be required of us to live in the presence of God.

"Keeping awake" also requires us to see, of course, the realities of living—sickness, death, injustice, poverty, war. The human response, my own included, is to sleep. Better to be unconscious than to face the problems which consciousness brings to our attention. Better even to feel bad about falling asleep than to stay awake. I imagine the disciples as bewildered, even despairing over their inability to do such a simple thing as stay awake; in Mark's Gospel, they apologize and then fall asleep all over again. "Despair," oddly enough, can indeed be a "comfort." Often we belittle ourselves, or say over and over again "why can't I do that right," aware, if only on some subconscious level, that we do not truly want to test ourselves, that we do not want to know the truth about ourselves.

On a larger scale, we would rather "weep so that we may be comforted," as Simone Weil understood, than face human misery head on and "undiluted." The suffering of others is, indeed, "intolerable," as Weil says. We choose sleep precisely because it is intolerable. "What could we do?" we rationalize, learning the circumnavigations of self-justification. Before Peter denies knowing Jesus, he warms himself by the high priests' fire; he is already asleep.

We sleep because the hour is always at hand. In a way the kingdom always-coming, always-here has come: the disciples feel the terror of choosing life or death, and there is no fear like the present. In the garden of Eden, in Moses's last speech to the Israelites in Deuteronomy, in all the Gospels, the choice is always life or death. Moses says, "I have set before you life and death, blessings and curses. Choose life so that you and your descendants may live, loving the Lord your God, obeying him, and holding fast to him" (Deuteronomy 30:19, 20).

In the New Testament, the disciples often ask Jesus when the kingdom of God will come. They are looking for a date—next Tuesday or six months from now or within the next five years. But Jesus reminds them over and over that the kingdom, paradoxically, is always-here, always-coming. Always-here if we choose life; always-coming because we are both terrified to choose life and are always learning how to choose life (as Auden said, we are always "becoming Christians").

When Adam and Eve are expelled from the garden, part of God's curse is death: "to dust you shall return." Dietrich Bonhoeffer understood that this curse is also a blessing. To Bonhoeffer, Adam is already dead before he dies. That is, Adam lives after the fall out of his own self; he has already experienced the death of being like God. The death of this death (living out of his own self) is the blessing Bonhoeffer rightly sees. It is also the promise and the terror of choosing Christ: you must lose your life to gain your life in Christ. The disciples flee instead. There is "no fear like the present" because in that moment we must choose life by choosing the death of our own self.

We sleep. We flee. I imagine this biblical moment as a moment in which the soul is both in torment and in paradise. Torment because it is so difficult to learn we do not rule because, as Bonhoeffer says, "we do not know the world as God's creation, and because we do not receive our dominion as God-given but grasp it for ourselves." Paradise because our "certain young man" is face to face with the one called Son of God with whom we know what it is like, once again, to be entirely ourselves, created in the image of God.

It is in this in-between that our unknown young man is each of us. To know ourselves in Christ is to choose. The *cost* of discipleship, as Bonhoeffer well knew, is to choose to die to our human ways of being in the world. The man in Mark, let's say, wants the peace of Christ but not the death it requires. If the Lenten season asks us, as Luke says, to pray earnestly, it also reveals that the cross and resurrection are two sides of the same coin. And so, like this man in the linen cloth, we twist away and flee, lost and safe once more in our darkness.

Mystery

"To treat life as less than a miracle is to give up on it."

—Wendell Berry

IN HIS BOOK *LIFE IS A Miracle,* Wendell Berry writes about that famous moment in Shakespeare's *King Lear* when Gloucester, blinded in retribution for his loyalty to Lear, has asked to be led to Dover where he intends to kill himself by leaping off the cliffs. His son Edgar tells Gloucester he is at the cliff's edge though in fact he is just back from it and, when Gloucester falls, he passes out, and reawakens at what he thinks is the bottom of the cliff, dismayed that he is still alive. It is then that Edgar says, "Thy life's a miracle. Speak yet again."

In his essay, Berry notes the obvious—that Gloucester and Lear are both guilty of hubris, of the "presumption" that life is "knowable, predictable, and within [their] control." But then Berry goes further, arguing that we "can give up on life . . . by presuming to 'understand' it—that is, by reducing it to the *terms* of our understanding and by treating it as predictable or mechanical." For Berry, to treat life as less than a miracle is an act of human will whereby the will contracts the world or appropriates the world to the will's understanding.

Our time is marked by our supreme belief in Enlightenment rationality. We are all too ready to say a word like "mystery" is a nostalgia; we limit the meaning of "mystery" to a quantity of the unknown, thereby opening the possibility that the inevitable acquisition of further knowledge will reduce that which is unknown and, in the future, erase the unknown entirely. A mystery is simply something to be solved—if not now, then later. But the biblical usage of "mystery" refers not to the quantity of the unknown but rather to the quality of the known; it refers to awe rather than ignorance. In that sense, mystery attests to the fact that no amount of research could make the creation or the life of Jesus or even the bond between husband and wife less mysterious. In its biblical sense, we can never be finished with mystery. The more we come to know it, the more we realize its difference from everything else. Mystery, like beauty, is not governed by concepts. It does not allow a conclusion. It goes beyond all the evidence.

And yet we have experience of such mystery, at least in part. In his book, *The Demon and the Angel,* the poet Ed Hirsch quotes a line that Lorca wrote at the bottom of one of his Buenos Aires drawings: "Only mystery enables us to live." Indeed. But as the poet Theodore Roethke knew, only those "who are willing to be vulnerable move among mysteries." I'd say the most necessary precondition for the experience of mystery is our understanding of ourselves as limited, of accepting, as Wendell Berry has said in his essay, "Two Minds," our "irreducible ignorance."

That's the rub: the great difficulty of living is uncertainty. Most of us prefer to move through the world unthinkingly secure in our accepted definitions of it. In order to feel comfortable or simply to go on functioning from day-to-day we act as if we know what our lives mean. In *Gravity and Grace*, the French philosopher Simone Weil said, "all sins are attempts to fill voids." As she saw it, we even go so far at times as to love what is imaginary—our own dreams and self-deceits, our ideas about life rather than life itself. And yet we live with a sense of dread in the back of our minds—those moments, which we know will disrupt our lives entirely (the death of someone we love, the sudden severe illness of ourselves or a friend, that late night phone call). Haven't we all felt how, at any moment, the ground on which we stand can open and, all too suddenly, we are falling into that dark abyss in which, once again, the meaning of our existence becomes a question we cannot fathom.

The book of Job records that dread. Thankfully, it's a *before* and *after* story: before and after the whirlwind from which God reveals his creation. From my perspective, it is a story that shifts both Job and the reader from a rational and calculative understanding of the world we live in towards one in which mystery lies at the center. For most of the book of Job, the character Job might be seen as a rationalist, committed to understanding the world in terms of his logical understanding: if I do good, I will be rewarded. Surely, he has been. As the story opens, the devout Job is one of the richest men in all of Uz.

But Job is pictured, at least in part, as a man that does good not out of love for the good, but because he fears what might happen if he does not. And then comes that Kafkaesque moment of dread: one day Job loses everything he has. Given his rational understanding of the world he lives in, and his conception of the God whom he's worshiped (someone just like Job but with some super powers to guard over him), Job cannot make sense of his suffering. He curses the day he was born, curses his life which can only be seen as a daily series of sufferings leading to oblivion, and wants, more than all else, a hearing in the courtroom of life, his God a judge who will adjudicate over his present life of suffering, find that he has done no wrong, and commute his sentence.

As readers we're aware of a central irony: Job's friends, who believe as Job does that God is just, the good are rewarded, and the evil punished, can only logically conclude that their friend must have done something wrong; but the frame tale that begins the story of Job gives us a knowledge of Job that they do not have: Job is guiltless, just as he claims. Nothing adds up as it's supposed to do. From the friends' perspective, Job is prideful because he will not admit what they would most like to hear—that he has done wrong—since such an admission of guilt on Job's part would put their worldview back in order. Job's suffering and his defiance has ruptured their very rational worldview: they have been successful because they have been good.

But from God's perspective—we learn this perspective when God speaks from the whirlwind—Job's pride has to do with the way he turned God into a larger version of himself, and the cosmos into a courtroom that worked according to human conceptions of right and wrong. When Job finally gets his hearing with God, God doesn't bother explaining anything at all. Instead of answering Job's central questions—Why am I suffering? Why do the wicked prosper?—God recapitulates his original creation in the form of a vision. That creation is staggering in its beauty, and in what I would call its random symmetry. It is a world of primal energy, independent of human beings, and a world which includes many things we might experience as terrifying: antelopes that are run down and eaten by lions but that do not see themselves as victims; a horse that exults because of the fierceness of battle; rain that falls where it does no good and water that takes on any number of forms, including forms like ice and hail that can wreak havoc on the human world. And that's just the beginning, since the "good" of creation also includes Behemoth and Leviathan, forces of such chaos only God can hold them at bay.

In short, the view from the whirlwind is clearly beyond human conceptions of good and evil.

Perhaps the greatest surprise of the story's ending is the fact that Job, who has filled the air around him with some of the most furious, courageous, tender, and exquisite language imaginable, who has cursed the day of his birth and asked every hard question we have ever thought to ask of God, falls silent. After the whirlwind, Job seems to comprehend immediately what we as readers struggle with—God's lack of answers to the questions Job himself has raised. Yet we sense what Job has been groping toward all along: that there are no causal explanations that can rationalize his plight.

As Northrop Frye has suggested in *Words with Power*, the God that speaks from the whirlwind prevents Job from looking back to a "chain of causation," that mainstay of both the friends and the pre-whirlwind Job, both of whom have tried to solve a mystery with the human logic of "this happened because. . . ." Instead of answering Job's logical questions, God presents Job with images so intense, Job, as he says, doesn't hear, but *sees*. As Job realizes *after* the whirlwind, he had previously only heard about God from Scripture and tradition. Now he sees "things too wonderful for me, which I did not know."

Job posited a God and a cosmos from his limited human position; he wanted a God who was just by human standards. What Job received, though he never even knew to ask, is the absolute justice of a creation that shouldn't be, but is, and is *good* (Genesis 1), despite its illogic and seeming capriciousness. The voice in the whirlwind enlarged Job's perspective by implicitly asking him: Does Job really want his moral sense projected on the universe? Does he want a God who is only a larger version of himself, a judge who rewards those who never realize virtue is its own reward? As it turns out in the end, both God and Job are "just" and that illogical fact defies the very logic by which Job and his friends have been operating.

The book of Job suggests that asking questions like "Why do I suffer?" or "Who is to blame?" are the rational mind's defense against the mystery of existence. We like to believe life is a problem to be solved. Our idea of success is something like a future where we will be able to control all those things we can't yet control, know all those things we, as yet, do not know. We like to believe, as Job's friends did, if we do x, we will get y.

What makes Job different from his friends is his openness; as Roethke put it, Job becomes someone who is "willing to be vulnerable" and so can "move among mysteries." If he shrinks the world to a courtroom by mistake, he also refuses the too-easy platitudes of his friends; if he once lived by fear, doing right because he was afraid of what might befall him and his family, he is also willing to admit that the good do suffer for no reason, the wicked often go unpunished and prosper, and, yes, the poor and afflicted are marginalized, made invisible for the ongoing comfort of the wealthy; and if he wanted a God who was something like a guardian angel to "fence" away all harm, he is quick to see the magnitude and magnanimousness of the God who speaks from the whirlwind.

In the vision of the whirlwind, Job finally realizes the limitations of the human intellect and how the very pursuit of the kind of logical world he wished for can lead to self-destruction. He becomes a kind of holy fool, that figure who questions the very ground we stand on, all our pet ideas and supposed understandings. As Abraham came to understand on his journey to Moriah, so Job realizes that to approach God, he must let go of all his ideas about God.

In her book, *Waiting for God,* Simone Weil asks that we "give up our imaginary position as the center, to renounce it, not only intellectually but in the imaginative part of our soul" so that we might "awaken to what is real and eternal, to see the true light and hear the true silence." Job does precisely this, admitting that his God cannot be someone who is created out of Job's own devising, for that God would be created out of malaise or complaint, out of desire or fear or hope. That God would be an idol. As Deuteronomy says, "the secret things belong to the Lord our God." When Job last speaks, saying, "now my eyes see you; therefore I repent in dust and ashes," he rectifies what he once turned upside down with his rational understanding. In chapter 30, verse 19, Job saw God as an enemy, the one responsible for turning him into no more than "dust and ashes." Now, after the whirlwind experience, Job acknowledges that he is "dust and ashes," that his narrow conception of justice, of right and wrong, had contracted God to his own human understanding. Job has seen the lioness and fierce horse in all their radiance and pure being; and now those final words are issued because he has, as Weil puts it, renounced his "imaginary position as the center." Job has been transformed and, now, out of love, not fear, gives himself whole-heartedly to God. In realizing his ignorance, Job's smallness and vulnerability open him to the vast mystery of God and creation.

three

On Poets and Poetry

The Otherworldliness
of Elizabeth Bishop

IN AN OFTEN-QUOTED letter to Anne Stevenson, Elizabeth Bishop writes that she "feels" that Robert Lowell and herself, "in very different ways, are both descendants from the Transcendentalists." What Bishop meant is open to question of course. On the one hand, those who read Bishop as a strictly secularist poet say (rightly) that Bishop didn't find correspondences between the natural and supernatural world. As she playfully acknowledges in poems like "The Fish," the fish, whose eyes just tilt back in its head, doesn't look back and acknowledge our stare; and in the much later "Poem," she notes that, while the Nova Scotia setting her uncle once painted and that she, too, has looked at and knows might be seen as corresponding "visions," "visions is too serious a word." No, what they see are simply "looks, two looks." In Bishop, "everything" is often connected only by "and" and "and," as she concludes in "Over Two Thousand Illustrations and a Complete Concordance."

On the other hand, there is the persistent feeling in Bishop's poems that the "interior" reveals, or at least shows itself, in more than just bird songs ("Cape Breton"), though even bird songs are something rather than nothing. And, the speaker's varied "looks" at the fish do lead to "rainbow, rainbow, rainbow," and in "Poem," Bishop's "look" at her uncle's painting brings the scene alive again in memory. In his very fine chapter on Elizabeth Bishop in *Reading and Writing Nature*, Guy Rotella suggests that Bishop's poems, though their descriptive aims are quite different from the transcendentalists, "nonetheless . . . frequently recall 'the correspondence game,' the process of moving from image to idea, from something seen to something known and believed." He adds, however, that the poems do so "in ways that question, thwart, and deny the analogies earlier poets claim." For Rotella, Bishop, like Frost and Stevens, "might be called a religious poet without religious faith."

I would say Bishop is a religious poet without an orthodox creedal religious faith. Yet, like her obsessive sandpiper, she is religiously faithful to "something, something, something"; I see that "something" in a number of ways: as something rather than nothing; as something that we can never fully know; as something akin to Stevens's "the thing itself" that is independent of our personal perspective, although our "seeing" can be and, is often, a matter of subjective imposition; as something that provides a communal experience, if only in our human knowing that some things restore that mysterious world in which we live, a world larger (and restorative precisely because it is larger) than any of our human attempts to enclose it in our understanding. In hopes of getting at the nature of the "religious" in Bishop and just how she might be a descendant from the Transcendentalists, I am going to juxtapose the Winander boy episode from Wordsworth's *Prelude*, Book V, beside Frost's "The Most of It" and both of those poems beside Bishop's "The Moose." While Bishop's work is shot through with doubt and skepticism, she is, for me, also a poet of wonder, and what she finds wonderful and "otherworldly" is existence itself (even if it can also be "awful"). For Bishop, our imagination is stretched to the utmost by the task of comprehending the strangeness of the world as it is.

Wordsworth's "There was a boy," originally written as a single poem and then placed in Book V of the *Prelude*, describes a kind of doubled experience. First, Wordsworth remembers a boy, friend to the cliffs and islands of Winander, and how he would make an "instrument" of his interwoven hands and whistle owl calls in the knowledge that the real owls will answer. And indeed they often did, in "long halloos and screams, and echoes loud, / redoubled and redoubled, concourse wild / of jocund din."

But there are times when their only reply is silence. Still, that silence affords a second, more profound experience: the boy's mind takes in the wider world of rocks and woods, and the nighttime sky's reflection in the lake, hinting at the imagination's formation by nature. The poem, perhaps an elegy to Wordsworth's own childhood, ends with him standing "mute" over the grave of the boy whose burial place lies within the vale of his birth. In the poem, we are left with the echoes of something lost, and yet still available to memory.

Wordsworth's poem is typical of the romantic lyric: it begins with the description of the scene and then gently moves to its revelations: first, that there is a connection, like Adam's naming of the creation, between the boy's whistles and the owls' "responsive" halloos—the natural world answers our longings for connection; secondly, though this physical responsiveness lasts only so long (twelve years before the boy is taken from his "mates," who can be both the cliffs and islands and his boy-hood friends), there is, to use Wordsworth's word from "Tintern Abbey," "recompense"—the deeper imaginative relation between the vale of Winander and the boy. In short, there are correspondences between the boy and the natural world, both physical and psychical, even if we acknowledge, as Wordsworth does, the boundaries of the self in relation to the indefinable natural world within which we live.

Some two hundred years later, Frost seemingly responds to this Wordsworth poem with "The Most of It." In Frost's poem a "He" (Adam) "thought he kept the universe alone." When Frost's "he" calls out to the world like the Winander boy, hoping to be met with "counter love, original response," all that comes back is the "mocking echo of his own" voice. "Nothing ever came" of his cries "unless" a powerful buck—nothing human and "someone else additional to him"—can be counted. The buck is all self-contained power and act: it "powerfully" appears, pushes the "crumpled water" out of its way as it swims across the lake, makes land "pouring like a waterfall," stumbles through the rocks on the speaker's shoreline, "forces" the underbrush, and disappears back into its forested world. And, as the "he" concludes—"that was all."

In his book, *Robert Frost: The Work of Knowing*, Richard Poirier warns that Frost's poem does not direct its irony toward the romantic attitude, "but toward a naïve version of it." The point is not simply that Wordsworth's Winander boy received a response whereas the "he" in Frost's poem did not. I agree. Frost's poem is a kind of companion piece to "Two Look at Two" where the overly romantic lovers, deluded by their own feelings, think they have experienced a deep connection to two deer. In "The Most of It," the "he," not getting the response he wants, doesn't make anything of the buck's appearance. Poirier's reading demonstrates the "he's" shortcomings, his inability to "keep" the world or make the most of it through "the [imaginative] work of knowing."

Still, there are some important differences between these poems of Wordsworth and Frost, and the way these poems point to Bishop's "The Moose." First, the relationship between the natural world and ourselves has been recast. In Frost, nature is no longer a friend, and no longer "responsive" in the same way. It is simply itself. The buck doesn't respond to the "he's" calls; and if its action (to cross the lake) is seen as a kind of response, the irony would be that the buck has been disturbed by the "he's" shouts. Secondly, though it is true, as Poirier says, that the "all" in the concluding phrase, and "that was all," does not mean that "all" is nothing, it does suggest that whatever the buck is and does, lies beyond our human ability to define it. That is, when we look to read the "book of nature," we don't find correspondence so much as the buck's power outstripping the "he's" ability to imagine it. And third, while the buck, unlike the owl or the Winander vale doesn't prompt a response in the "he" (because of his limitations to recognize the power of the buck or otherwise), the buck, does provoke a response in the reader, if only to acknowledge the power of the speaker's language regarding its otherness.

Bishop's "The Moose," composed of short, mostly three-beat lines, describes a bus journey from Nova Scotia to Boston. The poem falls roughly into three sections: the first traces the bus's route through small Nova Scotia towns as the day passes from morning to evening; the second takes place at night as the bus enters the New Brunswick woods and the passengers lie back and sleep, and the speaker, overhearing a conversation on the bus, falls into a "dreamy divagation"; the third describes the bus's encounter with a moose that has stepped out of the "impenetrable wood" and stopped the bus's movement for a time.

Looked at another way, the poem's three sections involve humankind's relation to the land, to one another, and to the otherworldly. And in a third take on the poem's three-part movement, we could say the poem moves from the anxiety of loss (the long goodbye of the first section to Nova Scotia) to a purgatorial-like dream state in which human sorrow is worked through and accepted as part of life rather than feared; and finally to the compensatory sight of the moose and the joy it brings.

In all three of my structural diagrams, we can see the structure of the Romantic lyric, and the genetic heritage of the Transcendentalists Bishop wrote of in her letter to Anne Stevenson. That is, the poem moves from landscape to meditation to revelation. And the speaker moves, as in the Romantic lyric, from a state of anxiety to one of joy, even if that joy is short-lived.

And yet, as with the Wordsworth and Frost poems, it is the differences that are important. In the first section of Bishop's poem, the Nova Scotia landscape is neither a "friend" or simply other, as I noted in Wordsworth and Frost. In Bishop, the natural world and the human world are both separate and intertwined. As the poem opens, Bishop's language and syntax about the tides maintains this doubleness:

From narrow provinces
of fish and bread and tea,
home of the long tides
where the bay leaves the sea
twice a day and takes
the herrings long rides.

where if the river
enters or retreats
in a wall of brown foam
depends on if it meets
the bay coming in,
the bay not at home.

The apposition in the third line makes the "long tides" part of the home of "narrow provinces"; and the tides going in and out seem to be human visitors. And yet the "herrings long rides" at sea are only *like* the speaker's long bus ride on land; the clapboard churches are "ridged" *like* clamshells, and while the bus has a "flank," its flank is of "blue, beat-up" metal. The human world domesticates the natural world as seen in the next stanzas—the planted "rows of maples," "the elms" that once canopied main streets—and, living within and alongside nature, we make our home.

And yet "home," "wherever that may be," as Bishop writes in "Questions of Travel," is always temporary, always being constructed. As "The End of March," another journey poem, makes clear, the "cryp-to-dream house" is only a dream, and our imaginary creations always run the risk of solipsism. For Bishop, the best response always seems to be a constant remaking of the self and home ("Home-made, home-made, aren't we all"—"Crusoe in England"). We remain the traveler whose travels are never complete. And so the movement in Bishop's poems is always away from and toward home. The "narrow" and domesticated Nova Scotia must be left behind; but there also must be a constant readi-ness for the ever-changing present and how it makes itself present to us.

The readiness is all, and in the second movement of "The Moose," Bishop's speaker undergoes the "hairy, scratchy, splintery" New Bruns-wick woods. Day has given way to night. As passengers lie back in their seats and fall asleep and others talk on into the night, the speaker falls into "auditory hallucination" as she listens to a conversation taking place "somewhere, / back in the bus":

Grandparents' voices

uninterruptedly
talking, in Eternity:
names being mentioned,
things cleared up finally;
what he said, what she said,
who got pensioned;

deaths and sicknesses;
the year he remarried;
the year (something) happened.
She died in childbirth.
That was the son lost
when the schooner foundered.

He took to drink. Yes.
She went to the bad.
When Amos began to pray
even in the stores and
finally the family had
to put him away.

"Yes . . . " that peculiar
affirmative. "Yes . . .
A sharp, indrawn breath,
half-groan, half-acceptance,
that means "Life's like that.
We know *it* (also death)."

In the back of her memory, those archetypal grandparents' voices
are heard mulling over the life of the village. The grandparents are lost
to eternity and perhaps only in Eternity (or at least in the eternity of
retrospection) are things "cleared up finally."

What's crucial is that the human sorrows narrated here are given
their due; there is both the bewilderment of our daily lives—all those
deaths, whether in childbirth, or by accident, or through sickness and
natural causes—and our responses to all that changes in our lives—
prayer, drink, madness. What's left is that "peculiar affirmative," "Yes."
Yes is "peculiar" because of the way New Brunswick Canadians literally
draw in their breath as they say "Yes"; and it is peculiar because it is
comprised of half-groans for all that we lose and cannot control and
half-acceptance because we come to learn that such loss makes life both
strange and precious.

The philosopher Simone Weil once said that the best proof of the good resides in the way the forces of entropy and destruction are kept at bay, if only barely. So, too, with Bishop's "yes," that seems to acknowledge "life's like that"—full of suffering and loss and death, and yet, as a counterbalance, life also brings comfort and peace and most of all the possibility of being "surprised," as Wordsworth knew, "by joy."

Like grace, joy seems to "come out of the impenetrable wood" on its own—it is not something that can be earned. Still, the speaker's acceptance of the "inscrutable" (another of Bishop's favorite words) world of suffering and loss prepares her for the moose; which is to say she doesn't react like the prototypical protective man who assures everyone that the moose is "perfectly harmless"; nor does she exclaim the obvious like the other passengers: that the moose is big, plain, and female.

No, the speaker tries at first to approach the moose that "looms" in the "middle of the road" through analogy: it is "high as a church, / homely as a house." The analogy hints at that strange conjunction of the domestic and spiritual, the homely and at-homeness, the ordinary and extraordinary that affords so much of the wonder in Bishop's world. Just consider the translucent grease-stained filling station; the pelicans that crash "like pickaxes" into the sea and even the dredge itself and its "untidy activity" in "The Bight"; or the wheelbarrows "plastered / with creamy iridescent coats of mail, / with small iridescent flies crawling on them" in "At the Fishhouses"; or the meadow, "which establishes its poverty in a snowfall of daisies" in "Cape Breton"; or the giant toad and giant snail; or Crusoe's knife; or the wasps' nest in "Santerem"; or the rainbow-bird in the bevel of a mirror ("Sonnet").

And, then, letting the moose take "her time," Bishop's speaker allows the moose to present itself, to make its presence felt. The moose lives in the duality of the transcendent here and now. The moose, pardon the pun, is "awe-full plain," both a moose and "grand, otherworldly." The two-word phrase is quite wonderful: "grand," a word first used by the woman who boarded the bus just before New Brunswick to describe the night, anchors the "otherworldly" to its homespun appreciation. That is, the moose is otherworldly in its this-worldliness, in its strangeness and in its strange appearance in the middle of the road; in the way it feels so outlandish and yet fits so perfectly with the New Brunswick woods, belonging to the place where it lives. This very real moose lives at the intersection of time and eternity, the speaker waking to it just as she told herself it was "all right now / even to fall asleep." When the quiet bus driver is moved to say, "Curious creatures," and "Look at that, would you," we are reminded that this creature that simply walked out of the woods is like life itself—"life's like that," the speaker had said earlier.

Unlike Frost's buck, Bishop's moose comes out of the "impenetrable wood"—not often and not for long—and allows itself to be seen. There is no veil to pierce as in Wordsworth, no hidden reality. But like Wordsworth's owls, though without the communication between boy and owls, the moose brings the "sweet sensation of joy." According to the speaker, everyone on the bus feels that joy. Despite her usual skepticism, despite her usual doubts, Bishop trusts in reality, the moose itself, the wonder of it, to present itself. It is a "grand" and startling gift, which she doesn't earn but receives, the "little that we get for free" ("Poem") which is and is "not much."

The ever-faithful Bishop knows and gives thanks in this poem for a moose that helps us see how a yesterday seemingly "impossible to lift" is "brought to today so lightly!" ("Five Flights Up"). And so should we.

Elizabeth Bishop and George Herbert
"Self-distaste" and Self-understanding

It's probably a hopeless matter, writing about favorite poems. . . .

—Robert Hass

FOR RICHARD HOWARD'S 1974 anthology, *Preferences: 51 American Poets Choose Poems from Their Own Work and the Past,* Elizabeth Bishop chose a favorite George Herbert poem, "Love Unknown," to juxtapose with her then as yet uncollected new poem, "In the Waiting Room." I was in graduate school, dividing my time between writing poems and studying them in earnest. Bishop and Herbert were my favorite poets and, as fate would have it, I was struggling in 1974 to describe, in a long overdue paper on Herbert, the tonality of many of Herbert's best known poems—that speaking voice which, say in "The Flower" or "Love 3," is utterly beguiling in its apparent simplicity and directness and yet has the power to turn the most innocuous word or phrase incandescent.

When, in 1974, I first read Bishop's "In the Waiting Room," I encountered that same power. How, I wanted to know (as both a writer and, I admit, a person with a religious temperament), did Bishop achieve such "mystery" (she'd say, "strangeness") in that series of why questions at the heart of "In the Waiting Room"? I still shiver at times over that first italicized *Why* and its tone of anxious, grave, bewilderment: "I felt: you are an *I* / you are an *Elizabeth*, / you are one of *them*. / *Why* should you be one, too?" Over twenty years later, I'm still trying to answer that question. While I'll look at the connections between Herbert's "Love Unknown" and Bishop's "In the Waiting Room," and while I'll look as well at Bishop's prose piece, "The Country Mouse," my abiding and central concern is still the way Bishop's poem enacts the radical and sudden disorientation which we all must undergo as we necessarily come to know the limits of our knowing.

As Bishop's "In the Waiting Room" opens, the speaker recalls how, while waiting for her aunt, she read a *National Geographic*. In a parenthetical aside, the speaker feels the need at this particular moment in the poem to declare "I could read." A whole interpretation of the poem lies within those parentheses for me. For isn't this poem about the discovery of the difference between the child's and the adult's understanding of what it means to read?

The peculiar slant of the poem—a child's voice filtered through the past-tense perspective of the adult—allows Bishop the many doublings of meaning that run throughout the poem. While the child may think reading involves only the words on the page, the older adult has learned, and now marks the moment of the poem as the beginning of that learning, that *reading* also means discovering the shock of those widening circles of unfamiliarity that the child encounters. When, at the end of the poem, the speaker comments, "Then I was back in it. / The War was on," we know and she knows that the singular "it" has a plurality of referents—the waiting room, her consciousness, the world that stretches from Worcester to Africa to "cold, blue-black space"—and that whatever order can be restored depends on mapping the various and variable constituent parts.

Thirteen years before "In the Waiting Room" was published, Bishop wrote about the incident in a prose piece, "The Country Mouse" (a piece that remained unpublished until 1984 when Robert Giroux gathered Bishop's uncollected prose together). Young Elizabeth is the "country mouse" whose Nova Scotia life was disrupted when her paternal grandparents took the six-year-old back to live with them in their cold, glum Worcester house. While "The Country Mouse" predominantly details the strain of young Elizabeth's divided loyalties—a Canadian child who had to memorize and daily recite, at her grandmother's feet, the verses of "The Star-Spangled Banner"—it culminates in three Wordsworthian "spots of time" in Worcester. All three moments involve a sudden irruption of painful self-consciousness. I want to concentrate on the first and third.

The first moment occurs when a friend, Emma, asks about Elizabeth's parents. Bishop writes,

> I said my father was dead; I didn't even remember seeing him.
> What about my mother? I thought for a moment and then I
> said in a *sentimental* voice: 'She went away and left me. She
> died, too.'

Of course, Bishop's mother is not dead; she's in a sanitorium at
the time suffering from another nervous breakdown. Looking back on
this childhood incident, the older Bishop doesn't know if she lied from
shame or for some "hideous craving for sympathy." But she does know
that the feeling that came over her "was only too real": that feeling was
"self-distaste" and Bishop was startled by the sudden discovery of her
"monstrous self."

The third moment occurs in the dentist's waiting room in Worcester.
The six-year-old Bishop has gone with her Aunt Jenny to the dentist
and, while she waits, she looks at a copy of the *National Geographic* for
February 1918. Here's how Bishop describes the scene:

> It was still getting dark early and the room had grown very
> dark. There was a big yellow lamp in one corner, a table
> with magazines, an overhead chandelier of sorts. There were
> others waiting, two men and a plump middle-aged lady, all
> bundled up. I looked at the magazine cover—I could read
> most of the words—shiny, glazed, yellow and white. The
> black letters said: FEBRUARY 1918. A feeling of absolute
> and utter desolation came over me. I felt . . . *myself*. In a few
> days it would be my seventh birthday. I felt *I, I, I,* and looked
> at the three strangers in panic. I was one of them, too, inside
> my scabby body and wheezing lungs. "You're in for it now,"
> something said. How had I got tricked into such a false posi-
> tion? I would be like that woman who smiled at me so falsely
> every once in a while. The awful sensation passed, then it
> came back again. "You are you," something said. "How
> strange you are, inside looking out. You are not Beppo [her
> dog], or the chestnut tree, or Emma, you are *you* and you
> are going to be *you* forever." It was like coasting downhill,
> this thought, only much worse, and it quickly smashed into
> a tree.

Why was I a human being? How to translate that feeling of "coast-
ing downhill" out of control and smashing into a tree—that is the task
Bishop takes up when she turns to this material thirteen years later in
"In the Waiting Room." How to capture that strange, awful (both in the
sense of horrible and awe-producing) sensation of that newly discovered
"I." As Bishop puts it, "*Why* was I a human being"?

In both "The Country Mouse" and "In the Waiting Room," the discovery of selfhood is a moment, in part, of "self-distaste," a moment when the child, like so many of George Herbert's speakers, discovers her own falseness and complicity. In her 1983 essay, "The Impersonal and the Interrogative in the Poetry of Elizabeth Bishop," Bonnie Costello first makes the connection between Herbert's "Love Unknown" and Bishop's "In the Waiting Room." She writes, "Like the speaker in George Herbert's 'Love Unknown,' which Bishop has juxtaposed with ["In the Waiting Room"], the young Elizabeth is made "new, tender, quick" through her sudden disorientation. It serves as a kind of baptism." Costello implies, of course, that the child's original orientation to the world is wrong-headed somehow. I'd say that the child, like Herbert's speaker who thought he knew what God wanted, has only a partial knowledge of what it means to "read." Young Elizabeth thinks she knows who she is; or, to put it another way, thinks she *can* know who she is.

The past tense perspective of both the Herbert and Bishop poems are important. In "Love Unknown," Herbert employs the past tense for its usual purpose: the speaker's "long and sad" tale told to his "deare friend" is a cautionary tale. The speaker "well remembers all" as well he should since, though he had in mind to bring some fruit to his Lord, his attempts amounted to a series of miscalculations and mishaps. Here's the poem:

> Deare Friend, sit down, the tale is long and sad:
> And in my faintings I presume your love
> Will more complie than help. A Lord I had,
> And have, of whom some grounds, which may improve,
> I hold for two lives, and both lives in me.
> To him I brought a dish of fruit one day,
> And in the middle plac'd my heart. But he
>   (I sigh to say)
> Lookt on a servant, who did know his eye
> Better than you know me, or (which is one)
> Then I my self. The servant instantly
> Quitting the fruit, seiz'd on my heart alone,
> And threw it in a font, wherein did fall
> A stream of bloud, which issu'd from the side
>
> Of a great rock: I well remember all,
> And have good cause: there it was dipt and dy'd,
> And washt, and wrung: the very wringing yet
> Enforceth tears. *Your heart was foul, I fear.*
> Indeed 'tis true. I did and do commit

Many a fault more then my lease will bear;
Yet still askt pardon, and was not deni'd.
But you shall heare. After my heart was well,
And clean and fair, as I one eventide
                         (I sigh to tell)
Walkt by my self abroad, I saw a large
And spacious fornace flaming, and thereon
A boyling caldron, round about whose verge
Was in great letters set AFFLICTION.
The greatnesse shew'd the owner. So I went
To fetch a sacrifice out of my fold,
Thinking with that, which I did thus present,
To warm his love, which I did fear grew cold.
But, as my heart did tender it, the man,
Who was to take it from me, slipt his hand,
And threw my heart into the scalding pan;
My heart, that brought it (do you understand?)
The offerers heart. *Your heart was hard, I fear.*
Indeed it's true. I found a callous matter
Began to spread and expatiate there:
But with a richer drug then scalding water
I bath'd it often, ev'n with holy bloud,
Which at a board, while many drunk bare wine,
A friend did steal into my cup for good,
Ev'n taken inwardly, and most divine
To supple hardnesses. But at the length

Out of the caldron getting, soon I fled
Unto my house, where to repair the strength
Which I had lost, I hasted to my bed.
But when I thought to sleep out all these faults
                         (I sigh to speak)
I found out that some had stuff'd the bed with thoughts,
I would say thorns. Deare, could my heart not break,
When with my pleasures ev'n my rest was gone?
Full well I understood, who had been there:
For I had giv'n the key to none, but one:
It must be he. *Your heart was dull, I fear.*
Indeed a slack and sleepie state of minde
Did oft possesse me, so that when I pray'd,
Though my lips went, my heart did stay behinde.
But all my scores were by another paid,
Who took the debt upon him. *Truly, Friend,*
For ought I heare, your Master shows to you
More favour then you wot of. Mark the end.

The Font did onely, what was old, renew:
The Cauldron suppled, what was grown too hard:
The Thorns did quicken, what was grown too dull:
All did but strive to mend, what you had marr'd.
Wherefore be cheer'd, and praise him to the full
Each day, each houre, each moment of the week,
Who fain would have you be new, tender, quick.

The speaker's plans—to bring his Lord a dish of fruit, a sheep, and later to rest so he might repair his strength to praise his Lord—are all frustrated. His "poor heart," with which the speaker brings his gifts, gets thrown into a bloody font and washed and wrung and later tossed into a scalding pan. When he tries to rest his heart, his bed becomes a bed of thorns.

But the speaker knows why. When his friend draws the moral from each narrated part, saying "Your heart was foul, I fear," "Your heart was hard, I fear," "Your heart was dull, I fear," the speaker quickly admits: "Indeed 'tis true." As Helen Vendler points out in her book on George Herbert, "it is characteristic of Herbert to recount his spiritual struggles in the past tense; they almost always are represented as having happened yesterday, so that the poem is giving today's view, a view tempered by knowledge of the purpose and result of each affliction." Though the speaker in Herbert's poem must, in some respect, tell this "sad tale" every day since all of us are "each day, each hour, each moment," prone to do the wrong thing, and must, as in Donne's great poem, "Batter my heart," be made "new, tender, quick" over and over again, the past tense perspective in Herbert assures us that our afflictions take place within a larger context. God's purposes, though we may not understand them from moment-to-moment, are always to mend what "we have marred," as the Deare Friend tells the speaker at the end of "Love Unknown."

Herbert's poems remind us, over and over, how, even when we think we are acting most righteously and meekly and humbly, our self-congratulating self is winding its ways into our actions. I think Bishop recognizes and feels sympathy with Herbert's self-conscious understanding of what she called her "monstrous self" in "The Country Mouse."

"In the Waiting Room" traces, I think, that moment when the child, who thought she was so different from the adults in the dentist's office, so different even from her own "foolish Aunt," must experience how, however "unlikely," she is "one of *them*." Yet Bishop's past-tense perspective has none of the assurances of Herbert's—and therein lies part of the poem's strangeness. We expect a past-tense poem to provide a comfortable distance from the narrated events; often the stance of the speaker is the one we encountered in Herbert: this or that happened but now I know why. But in the same way Bishop conflates child and adult in "In the Waiting Room," she conflates past and present. The reader moves inside the speaker's memory as the speaker moves inside the *National Geographic* volcano so that the child's experience of sudden disorientation is also the reader's. As we read, we confront those same unanswerable whys. Or, to put it another way, we hear them again for the first time with the ears of a child.

In the epigraphs to her collection *Geography III* that immediately precede its first poem, "In the Waiting Room," we're given a set of child-like questions and answers from a child's primer in geography. Here's a sample:

> *What is geography?*
> *A description of the earth's surface.*
> *What is the earth?*
> *The planet or body on which we live.*

The answers are a child's answers, a way of beginning with a complex subject. As readers of *Geography III*, we immediately suspect that those answers are insufficient when, on the facing page, Bishop provides a verse paragraph of unanswered questions:

> In what direction is the Volcano? The Cape? The Bay? The
> Lake? The Strait? The Mountains? The Isthmus?
> What is in the East? In the West? In the South? In the North?
> In the Northwest? In the Southeast? In the Northeast? In the
> Southwest?

The first unanswered question, then, in *Geography III* is: "In what direction is the Volcano?" In the context of the geography primer, the answer might be simple. But in the context of "In the Waiting Room," the answers are many and complex. The volcano is both inside the *National Geographic* and inside the mouth of Aunt Consuelo when her pain spills over in a cry, a cry which, of course, Elizabeth recognizes as her own as well. The volcano is at once "black and full of ashes" and spilling over "in rivulets of fire" just as the pictures in the *National Geographic*, at first tame and civilized (Osa and Martin Johnson in lace and riding boots), soon spill over in "babies with pointed heads" and "black, naked women with necks / wound round and round with wire."

As Brett Millier and others have pointed out, the perspective is constantly shifting at the poem's opening—Elizabeth is in Worcester, but outside in the waiting room. Once inside the *National Geographic* Elizabeth is forced outside into "blue-black space" through the "oh! of pain" that come simultaneously from inside the dentist's office (her aunt's voice) and outside in the waiting room (from inside young Elizabeth).

Bishop's point is clear: nothing is ever one thing. The boundaries between inside and outside, between the familiar and unfamiliar, between what we call our world and other, are always artificial, self-created and often self-willed, and always, always fluid and changing, like knowledge which is "flowing and flown" in "At the Fishhouses." Still, though the point may be clear, our experience of the poem is constantly unsettling. We know the poem is a recollection; and we presume the speaker is the older Elizabeth, not the child that's nearly seven. Yet when we try to discriminate between the child's voice and the adult's there is very little to go on. Like third-person fiction which immediately moves inside the protagonist's head and stays there, we have, as readers of "In the Waiting Room" no authorial perspective.

And consider how the poem skips along in loose trimeter, even as it recollects those horrifying naked breasts. Even the syntax and grammar are unsettling:

> The waiting room
> was full of grown-up people,
> arctics and overcoats,
> lamps and magazines.

Is the waiting room full of grown-ups and boots and overcoats and lamps and magazines or are grown-ups synonymous with "arctics and overcoats, lamps and magazines" in the child's mind? Certainly one of the masterful feats of "In the Waiting Room" is Bishop's careful control of perspective. On the one hand, she keeps her poem from childishness and sentimentality by using the past tense (which maintains the distance between the speaker and child, and the reader and the child). As adults and readers of the poem, we are able to observe the child's struggles with the volcanic world of the *National Geographic* and her own female body; we see, too, how the familiar turns suddenly unfamiliar and how the child struggles to map this unfamiliar terrain: by comparing, say, the exotic neck decoration of the African women to a common light bulb or by creating boundaries between herself and the magazine when she notes the cover's yellow margins and date.

On the other hand, as I've noted, the poem constantly pushes us inside the child's experience, blurring the boundaries between adult speaker and child. When the "oh! of pain" erupts from inside the dentist's office, the reader, like the child who believed she could stand outside the event—"I wasn't at all surprised; / even then I knew she was / a fool-ish, timid woman"—is suddenly caught up in the confusion. At first we assign the cry of pain to Aunt Consuelo; then we're not so sure:

> What took me
> completely by surprise
> was that it was *me*:
> my voice, in my mouth.
>   Without thinking at all,
> I was my foolish aunt,
> I—we—were falling, falling

What's happened? Has the child let out an "oh! of pain," horrified as she is by those "awful, hanging breasts"? Have both Aunt Consuelo and the young Elizabeth cried out? Even if we're able to say in the end that the child recognizes the "family voice" in Aunt Consuelo's cry of pain, and thus her own voice as well, the momentary confusion is crucial. For suddenly, we, too, are falling—not with the child necessarily nor in the same way as the child, but falling, nevertheless, into the tumble of questions that immediately follow.

And isn't that the point? When Bishop collapses the distance be-tween reader and child, she short-circuits our role as detached interpreter of the child's experience. The roll-call of questions, questions left unan-swered because they are unanswerable, takes the reader "completely by surprise." *Why* should we be who we are? For those of us who love this poem, the effect of this *Why* is almost preternatural. Just as the child, once secure in her simple definitions—she was in Worcester, in a wait-ing room, it was winter, and she *could* read—is suddenly confronted by the "unlikeliness" of her likeliness to others, by the worlds-upon-worlds that she now must learn to read, we, too, (who move through the world secure in our accepted definitions of it) are confronted by those most basic questions which somehow we never really answered. Why should we be who we are? And what constitutes who we are? And, why, oh why have we come to be here?

What Bishop captures and helps us experience is the shock of being alive: isn't it amazing that there is that, and not just me. And, even more remarkably, there is something rather than nothing. The experience of the young Elizabeth is preconceptual—she is "taken" (both carried off and astonished) and "without thinking at all," she *is* her foolish aunt (notice the missing "like"). Like Robinson Crusoe finding footprints in the sand, the child is startled to find there are others and otherness in the world. Even more startling, perhaps, is the sense that because there is other, because there is that which is "not me," there is also me:

> you are an *I*,
> you are an *Elizabeth*,
> you are one of *them*.

The fact that the child has an individual identity that separates her from others, but also connects her to others, since in recognizing who she is, she recognizes others are just like her, is, as Bishop says, one of the strangest things that can happen. Though our experience as readers is not the child's, we, too, are brought to a place inside the poem where something strange happens: we hear those fundamental questions at the heart of the poem as if for the first time.

We arrive with the child at this most "unlikely" place because we make, in our own ways, the same fundamental mistake as the child. We think we know how to read. We act as if we know—because we must go on functioning in the day-to-day world—what our lives mean. As in Bishop's poem, and Herbert's, it usually takes a volcanic eruption or a scalding pan to disrupt our complacency and indifference.

Consider how a death of someone we love or a sudden severe illness of a friend brings us back to the starting point: for what purpose do I exist? For me, the great power of Bishop's "In the Waiting Room" is this: it enacts that moment when we experience the abyss which is always just underfoot. Haven't we all felt how, at any moment, the ground on which we stand can open and we, too, fall into that "cold, blue-black space" in which our existence becomes a question to ourselves?

Think of how Bishop enacts for us the changed reality of the child. At the opening of the poem the waiting room is described matter-of-factly: lamps and boots, grownups, tables with magazines. When the child falls into the blue-black space that opens under her feet, that same commonplace scene becomes intensely focused—so much so the child can only afford a "sidelong glance." In this later scene, the child doesn't look at the objects in the waiting room; rather the objects force their reality upon the child. Elizabeth sees the same "trousers and skirts and boots" but the significance of their realness is something altogether different. Now that same waiting room forces a new reading on the child:

> What similarities—
> boots, hands, the family voice
> I felt in my throat, or even
> the *National Geographic*
> and those awful hanging breasts—

held us all together
and made us all just one?

The experience the child undergoes—and we, too, as readers—involves our coming to know the limits of our knowing. For Herbert in "Love Unknown" and for Bishop in "In the Waiting Room" such an experience necessarily entails a moment when we suffer a radical and sudden disorientation: what we thought we knew is suddenly and deeply called into question. As Bishop painfully understood, such moments often involve the bitter feeling of "self-distaste": Elizabeth comes to know she is her "foolish aunt." To be made "new, tender, quick," as Herbert says, we must (though, of course, that remaking takes place over and over again), we must first come to a moment when, like young Elizabeth, we become a question to ourselves. In Worcester, Massachusetts, where Elizabeth Bishop lies buried, she first came to "read" the vast and multi-faceted world she would travel and map in her poems.

On George Herbert's "Jordan 2"

When first my lines of heav'nly joys made mention,
Such was their lustre, they did so excell,
That I sought out quaint words and trim invention;
My thoughts began to burnish, sprout, and swell,
Curling with metaphors a plain intention,
Decking the sense, as if it were to sell.

Thousands of notions in my brain did runne,
Off'ring their service, if I were not sped:
I often blotted what I had begunne;
This was not quick enough, and that was dead.
Nothing could seem too rich to clothe the sunne,
Much lesse those joyes which trample on his head.

As flames do work and winde, when they ascend,
So did I weave my self into the sense.
But while I bustled, I might heare a friend
Whisper, *How wide is all this long pretense!*
There is in love a sweetnesse readie penn'd;
Copie out onely that, and save expense.

WHAT I LOVE ABOUT THIS poem (and its companion, "Jordan
1") is the dilemma of writing religious verse that it enacts. The
past tense here signals both an acknowledgment of past errors and hides
an ongoing struggle. Herbert wants, like every poet, to be seen as a good
poet who knows his craft; he wants others, especially God, to see both
his imaginative inventiveness and his ability to wield language. He wants
to capture the amplitude and richness of his experience with language
equal to the task.

And yet. And yet he has learned to suspect those very desires. And well he should. If Herbert knows he must love the very language he employs to speak about God to write a good poem, he also knows how that very language may be fraught with pride and self-interest, may be the very thing that gets in the way of God. Herbert's vexing, great question is—how does he represent the felt reality of God with language that can only, being bound by the writer's own finite limitations, "weave [his] self into the sense"?

Over and over in his poems, Herbert declares that too much artfulness only "curl[s] with metaphors a plain intention." He asks, to create an authentic hymn of praise "must all be veiled, while he that reads, divines / Catching the sense at two removes" (from "Jordan 1")? The solution should be easy: "There is in love a sweetness ready penned: / Copie out only that, and save expense." But, the instruction he hears—to use the words of God that are "already penned" in the Bible—is more complicated than it seems: if Herbert substitutes the words of the Bible for his own words then the result may well be sufficient for God but insufficient for a good poem. And how does a poet, who loves the feeling of the way words "sprout" more words so feverishly the poet's hand can hardly record all those ideas that are "off'ring their service," simply copy out only that which is both readily available and already been penned.

Consider how alive Herbert's language is (in stanza one and two), how intricate the syntax, when he is admitting to the errors he has committed. Part of him wants to believe that the richness of God demands an equally appropriate richness of language. But that belief may only be the intricate-egotistic-poetic-self whispering in Herbert's ear—as the poet quietly admits in the buying and selling undertones of the diction at the end of stanza one.

At the heart of this poem, then, is the contradiction at the heart of all spiritual writing and perhaps writing in general—how can the poet be fully present, completely "there" in the poem, employing his/her love for words and craft, and, at the same time, disappear? How, on the one hand, can the writer, who wants to disappear, escape finally his own "long pretense"? And, on the other hand, what writer wants to "save expense," when it is those very riches the writer loves to expend?

Stanley Kunitz
The Agony of Coming Alive

MY OWN CONNECTION TO Stanley Kunitz's poetry is quite simple: I love the spirit of his work; I love the way he honors living and dying. Speaking about his own long life of writing shortly before he died, Kunitz reminds us that a writer's work is "not an expression of the desire for praise, or recognition, or prizes, but the deepest manifestation of [one's] gratitude for the gift of life."

Writing for Stanley Kunitz was an act of gift-giving, the poem a gift he made to the world in acknowledgment of the gift he had been given. Kunitz knew the paradox of such giving: he knew that he "must perish into work," exhausting himself in the act of poem-making; and he knew that if he succeeded in perishing, he would put himself in touch with that wellspring of poetry, what he once called "innocence in the arts." In the "Reflections" Kunitz added to his *Collected Poems* (2000) he wrote: "At the core of one's existence is a pool of energy that has nothing to do with personal identity, but that falls away from the self, blends into the natural universe. Man has only a bit part to play in the marvelous show of creation."

Gratitude. It lies at the heart of Kunitz's work and what I love about his work. But we should not forget how hard-won Stanley Kunitz's gratitude truly was. Of our major poets, only Elizabeth Bishop matches his slow, thrifty production; as Kunitz has put it, he wrote only those poems that forced themselves into being. Kunitz also shares with Bishop a very troubled start to life. In a 1971 interview with Selden Rodman, Kunitz talked about his past: "Perhaps my father, who killed himself six weeks before I was born, came from East Prussia; I've never known much about him because my mother made it a forbidden subject . . . not even his name could be mentioned. . . . I was farmed out, or in the hands of nursemaids;

I was lonely and fatherless. . . . My two sisters died young. Mother was just forty when I was born. When I was eight she married again. My stepfather taught me most of what I know about love and gentleness. . . . When he died in my fourteenth year, my world was shattered."

Of course, anyone who knows Kunitz's work comes to know the centrality of the missing father who is sought continuously and who responds with the "ignorant hollow" of his face rather than the fatherly guidance that is so wanted. Out of this past, and out of the need to find a way to contain and transform that past comes the title of this piece. "The Agony of Coming Alive" is a phrase of Kunitz's that appears in a review of Theodore Roethke's book, *The Lost Son*. Roethke, whom Kunitz called a "poet of transformations," was a friend and correspondent of Kunitz and a poet who, like Kunitz, wanted (as Gregory Orr has pointed out) to express his deepest feelings towards his father in poems that were too "personal" for the times. I think Roethke, like his own poetic model Yeats, wrote poems that gave Kunitz the necessary "masks" (to use Yeats's word) for a poetry of transformation, a poetry that could find those images and phrases that transform one's personal life into myth. Kunitz would have certainly agreed with Yeats that "all that is personal soon rots."

But while he always feared self-indulgence and mere confessionalism, he also knew that he needed to make art out of his very personal and complicated past, a past that left him with his fair share of hang-ups and guilts. In his essay, "Seedcorn and Windfall," from his book *A Kind of Order, A Kind of Folly*, Kunitz notes that originality for a poet has to do with his or her unique past. The poet who seeks originality will fail. But the poet who "tracks down those key images which will unlock his deepest and most secret reality" will discover the originality of a past which is different from any other's past. Unlocking that "deepest and most secret reality" involves, necessarily, the "agony of coming alive."

Kunitz's phrase "track down" captures the long and tiring process of composition that he often talked about. As he knew, no poem worth writing "lies easy in the mind for the picking." From the start, Kunitz stood against an impersonal theory of poetics, despite the formal and knotted quality of his earlier work. For him, there was an "indispensable encounter between the artist and his medium" that determines the poet's choices of word, image, sound, voice. Poem writing is a kind of "testing-tree." The poet, for Kunitz, must "dare to submit [himself] to the ordeal of walking through the fire of selfhood into a world of archetypal forms" ("A Kind of Order").

In his essay "The Search for a Style" Kunitz wrote:

> In the best poetry of our time—but only the best—one is
> aware of a moral pressure being exerted on the medium in the
> very act of creation. By 'moral' I mean a testing of existence
> at its highest pitch—what does it feel like to be totally one's
> self?; an awareness of others beyond the self; a concern with
> values and meanings rather than with effects; an effort to tap
> the spontaneity that hides in the depths rather than foams
> at the surface; a conviction about the possibility of making
> right and wrong choices, even symbolic choices. Lacking this
> pressure, we are left with nothing but a vacuum occupied by
> a technique.

As Kunitz knew, "talent without character is the worst kind of
curse." Character is what Kunitz forged over his long career.

But before I talk about some of his poems, I want to spell out both
what Kunitz means and what I mean by character. For me, a discussion
of character begins with the artistic connection between Kunitz and his
true poetic father, John Keats. What Keats faced—the loss of his father
at an early age, the loss of one brother to an early death and another
to America—is not unlike Kunitz's own life story. It is no accident that
Kunitz edited a volume of Keats's poems and wrote an extended essay on
"The Modernity of Keats."

Both Keats and Kunitz desire the "music of transformation," a music that is willing to affirm "the inviolable Self consolidated against the
enemies within and without that would disperse it" (both phrases are
from Kunitz's essay "The Modernity of Keats"). What Kunitz grasped
in Keats was the necessity of "Negative Capability" for the kinds of poems Kunitz wanted to write. Writing to his brothers about Shakespeare,
who he had been reading, Keats argues that it is Shakespeare's enormous
capacity for "Negative Capability"—"when a man is capable of being
in uncertainties, mysteries, doubts without any irritable reaching after
fact and reason"—that lies behind his greatness. For Kunitz, the "spiritual testimony" that Keats's work makes and the "spontaneity of Keats's
mind"—aspects of Kunitz's own work that I treasure—have all to do
with Keats's capacity for Negative Capability.

Keats produced a language which could hold inside itself the contradictions of life without any irritable reaching out after fact and reason. Keats was always trying to escape from "fixity" and his notion of
poetical character which must enjoy "light and shade . . . live in gusto,
be it fair or foul, high or low, rich or poor" aligns itself quite well with a

passage from Kunitz's essay "A Kind of Order": "That order is greatest which holds in suspension the most disorder; holds it in such precarious balance that each instant threatens its overthrow. In life and in art, consistent with the precept of Paul Tillich, 'the self-affirmation of a being is the stronger the more non-being it can take into itself.'" The best poets polarize the conditions of order and disorder inside themselves without the aid of explanations or theories. In that sense, Kunitz can say, "With Keats the ordeal of the life becomes sacred for poetry." And we can hear in that phrase what it means to "walk through the fires of selfhood," to turn one's life into a poem, as Kunitz, following Keats, tried to do.

I want to look now at a little selection of Kunitz's poems which I think are pivotal poems in his poetic career and mark decades of his 100-year lifespan. I've chosen to touch on a few poems from the thirties, forties, and fifties—"Change," "Goose Pond," "The End of Summer" and "Father and Son"—and then move to a couple of poems, "The Portrait" and "The Testing-Tree," from Kunitz's pivotal 1971 book, *The Testing-Tree*. Finally I'll look at "Snakes of September," "Passing Through," and "Touch Me," poems from Kunitz's seventh, eighth, and ninth decades. My focus will be on the extraordinary way Kunitz's work is and is not confessional. As Gregory Orr has put it, Stanley Kunitz has always tried to turn his "life into legend." Kunitz is primarily a poet of the dramatic lyric and what he dramatizes is Keats's "vale of soul-making," those fires of selfhood in which we quest for love, for authenticity, and for the intensity of being itself.

The first poem in Stanley Kunitz's *Collected Poems* is "Change"; in it, Kunitz announces what will be an abiding concern—the endless transformations of the self which is always in a state of "becoming." Here are the key lines: "late and soon / Becoming, never being, till / Becoming is a being still." From "Change" to "Touch Me" (the last poem in the *Collected*), Kunitz has traced his becomings. And if becoming is an endless task it also involves, as Kunitz's play on words makes clear, "being still"—both the end of life and being nonetheless. That is, the stillness of being drives all those transformations until the self arrives possibly at "being still."

But the "agony of coming alive" lies precisely in those transformations of becoming. The justly famous poem, "Father and Son" from the forties book, *Passport to the War*, charts the path "down sandy road / Whiter than bone-dust" towards the "secret odor of ponds," where life and death commingle and where Kunitz must "find the furies that made him man" (as he puts it in the later "Goose Pond"). If we follow Kunitz's lead regarding those "key images" of the past, it's clear that they always have something to do with doors and thresholds, with borderline places where Kunitz must work out his relationship to the absent father and the mother who has suppressed the past in a stinging silence. Or to put it less psychologically, the self seeking identity must remain in the tension of those places that both conceal and reveal.

"End of Summer," the poem that precedes "Goose Pond" in *This Garland, Danger, Selected Poems, 1928–1958*, concerns the discovery of a moment when the "agony of coming alive" makes itself felt in a premonition. The "End of Summer" registers that ages-old premonition of the coming winter while summer is still in force. Yet while there are the sounds of migrating geese as summer's blue continues to "[pour] into summer's blue," Kunitz's agitation has more to do with a "perturbation" of the self who knows the year has gone by "unloved." Now those hints of winter announce an end to "that part of [his]life." What I particularly like about this poem is the way it captures the strangeness of those ordinary moments when we realize, even if subconsciously, that something has changed in us. Here it is:

> An agitation of the air,
> A perturbation of the light
> Admonished me the unloved year
> Would turn on its hinge that night.
>
> I stood in the disenchanted field
> Amid the stubble and the stones,
> Amazed, while a small worm lisped to me
> The song of my marrow-bones.
>
> Blue poured into summer blue,
> A hawk broke from his cloudless tower,
> The roof of the silo blazed, and I knew
> That part of my life was over.
>
> Already the iron door of the north
> Clangs open: birds, leaves, snows
> Order their population forth,
> And a cruel wind blows.

"The Portrait," a pivotal poem from his 1971 book *The Testing-Tree*, crystallizes many of the earlier poems' search for the father and identity, a search begun with "Father and Son" (1944) and picked up later by the poem called "The Knot." "The Portrait" is also the first poem to mention his father's death as a suicide and most importantly it is written with the simplicity and understatement that is characteristic of Kunitz's later work. For me, *The Testing Tree* is the book that first announces Kunitz's voice, his particular stamp on experience that can be heard in the cadences of his syntax.

"The Portrait" is composed of four sentences and it traces four actions of his mother: never forgiving the speaker's father; never speaking his name; ripping up the picture the son finds of his father; and slapping the speaker in the face. Kunitz, who was shifting at this time from predominantly rhymed formal verse to free verse, uses his line to add one new piece of information per line. Crucial information is beautifully withheld and paced: "My mother never forgave my father," the poem begins. For what?—"for killing himself" the next line finally gives us matter of factly. And for killing himself at "such an awkward time" the third line adds and we ask "why awkward" (because of another woman; because she was pregnant with the speaker; because, as biographies tell us, their business was failing)? But before we can say all of the above, the fourth line adds "and in a public park" and the fifth "that spring," piling on the ironies of public shame and a denial of what should be a life-producing season.

Kunitz is a master not only of what is said, but also of what remains unspoken. As Kunitz will say in "The Testing-Tree," "Never try to explain." We're never told that the speaker's mother doesn't tell the speaker his father's name once she is handed the picture the boy discovers. We're told instead that "she ripped it into shreds and slapped [him] hard." The name remains taboo but magical, a ghost name, a possibly healing as well as traumatizing name, and a name, which unspoken, still leaves its mark on the boy, now man's face: "In my sixty-fourth year / I can feel my cheek / still burning." Consider how that last sentence goes on multiplying its emotional effects.

The title poem of "The Testing-Tree" makes explicit what has been implicit up to now: that to feel what it "feels like to be totally one's self" requires one to "go / through dark and deeper dark / and not to turn." The paradox of life is that the heart "lives by breaking." Any attempt to explain this paradox, to understand the psychological drama of mother/father/son would be to reduce the complexities of human experience to a false simplicity. The "furies that made him man"—a lost house, a lost father, a sister who went off and "nothing [came] back," a mother who would not talk of his father—must be faced and suffered. The heart can only be nourished by opening itself. Such openness involves suffering and vulnerability and the acceptance of the conditions of being. The crucible where the self is made is a place where all the "elements of disorder" must be admitted and held in tension with whatever order is to be created.

The next two poems are from Kunitz's 1985 collection *Next-To-Last Things*, my favorite of his books. The first poem is called "Snakes of September" and I want to consider how the poem answers Kunitz's notion that "poetry is ultimately mythology, the telling of stories of the soul." The soul in this poem is at the crossroads of two seasons and of what can be known. The poem is about one of the most basic human dramas: the quest for love and for what I earlier called the intensity of being. Consider:

All summer I heard them
rustling in the shrubbery
outracing me from tier
to tier in my garden,
a whisper among the viburnums,
a signal flashed from the hedgerow,
a shadow pulsing
in the barberry thicket.

Now that the nights are chill
and the annuals spent,
I should have thought them gone,
in a torpor of blood
slipped to the nether world
before the sickle frost.
Not so. In the deceptive balm
of noon, as if defiant of the curse
that spoiled another garden,
these two appear on show
through a narrow slit
in the dense green brocade
of a north-country spruce,
dangling head-down, entwined
in a brazen love-knot.
I put out my hand and stroke
the fine, dry grit of their skins.
After all,
we are partners in this land,
co-signers of a covenant.
At my touch the wild
braid of creation
trembles.

How casually and astonishingly the poem slides from the literal to the mythic. The snakes, which were heard, but never quite seen—a "whisper," a "signal flashed," a "shadow pulsing"—during the summer months are now brazenly visible in September when they should be slipping to the "nether world." Kunitz slides the poem into myth with an "as if": these snakes "appear on show" "as if defiant of the curse / that spoiled another garden." Here they are: two September snakes "entwined" in a "love-knot." Kunitz has two choices: to banish them from his garden; to welcome them. He chooses the latter, recognizing as he strokes the "fine, dry grit of their skins" that he and the snakes are "partners in this land, / co-signers of a covenant."

In many of these later poems, Kunitz recognizes the "gods in exile"—snakes, raccoons, a beached whale. These gods remind us of the intensity of being, of "pure energy incarnate," to use Kunitz's phrase for the Wellfleet whale and they "ask of us / not sympathy, or love, / or understanding, / but awe and wonder." The September snakes are our partners in creation; the covenant all have signed is with the integral rightness of creation and the blessing of the vitality of being. In Kunitz's little story, the curse is reversed when we see ourselves as part of the "braid of creation" and as partners in its continuance. Awe and wonder. Only in that posture does the self experience both its own impermanence and the essence of being ultimately shared by all of us. Only then can the "braid of creation / tremble" at our astonished touch.

The second poem I want to consider is the title poem, "Passing Through." Kunitz wrote the poem on the occasion of his seventy-ninth birthday. In the poem, Kunitz addresses his wife whom he says is the first person to "bully" him into celebrating his birthday. Here's the opening stanza:

> Nobody in the widow's household
> ever celebrated anniversaries.
> In the secrecy of my room
> I would never admit I cared
> that my friend were given parties.
> Before I left town for school
> my birthday went up in smoke
> in a fire at City Hall that gutted
> the Department of Vital Statistics.
> If it weren't for a census report
> of a five-year-old White Male
> sharing my mother's address
> at the Green Street tenement in Worcester

I'd have no documentary proof
that I exist. You are the first,
my dear, to bully me
into these festive occasions.

Two of my colleagues at Holy Cross who taught a course on Worcester and Worcester poets tell me that Stanley Kunitz's birth certificate is still on record at City Hall. It never went up in smoke as the poem asserts. Obviously, Kunitz is pushing the facts into myth, in this case the myth of existence. What does it mean to exist, the poem playfully puts before us. On the one hand, does the "I" who is Stanley Kunitz become a non-entity because birthdays and anniversaries were forbidden in Kunitz's mother's household? Or because documentary proof of his existence is almost nil. Or is that "I" nothing more than a borrowed handful of dust as the second stanza suggests. Here's the second and concluding stanza:

Sometimes, you say, I wear
an abstracted look that drives you
up the wall, as though it signified
distress or disaffection.
Don't take it so to heart.
Maybe I enjoy not-being as much
as being who I am. Maybe
it's time to practice
growing old. The way I look
at it, I'm passing through a phase:
gradually I'm changing to a word.
Whatever you choose to claim
of me is always yours;
nothing is truly mine
except my name. I only
borrowed this dust.

As you can see, the poem explains why such celebrations are not necessary and, for good measure, gets at that old question: who am I? Kunitz's answer is much like the answer of his beloved Keats, though the utter directness of the speaking voice reminds me of George Herbert and of the way Herbert's poems are both personal and impersonal, the poem both literal and a parable, a story which the "I" is telling and a story which is everyman's.

I'm astonished over and over by the way this poem joins—seamlessly—the personal and the impersonal. There's the touching personalness of a poem so directly addressed to his wife. "Don't take it so to heart," Kunitz casually responds to his wife's anger over the distracted look on his face. And later, "Whatever you choose to claim / of me is always yours." Here's a man who knows what's being given away at every moment in a marriage: whatever you need of me is always yours. Nothing less. And yet there is also the full and equally casual acknowledgment that the enjoyment of giving himself away to a loved wife is only part of what existence demands. Not-being must be enjoyed as well since "who I am" is, in the end, only borrowed dust. That impersonal knowledge requires deliberate practice since the "art of losing" is always hard to master. For Kunitz, existence is a series of necessary metamorphoses, which if undergone with exacting truth, brings us to our own nothingness. Kunitz also acknowledges his life as a writer in this poem: he is passing through, "changing to a word," as if the writer's one consuming task should be the exchange of his name for an identity-less word that names the continual movement between being and non-being.

The last poem I want to look at was written when Kunitz was ninety years old. It is called "Touch Me" and is from *The Later Poems, New and Selected* published in 1995. Once again the poem is addressed to his wife. Once again, the poem positions itself between seasons, this time summer and fall, the speaker remembering, as he listens to a storm outside his house, how that afternoon he kneeled in his garden and listened to crickets. The poem begins with a line Kunitz recalls from a poem he wrote in 1958, nearly forty years earlier, called "As Flowers Are." Here's the poem:

> *Summer is late, my heart.*
> Words plucked out of the air
> some forty years ago
> when I was wild with love
> and torn almost in two
> scatter like leaves this night
> of whistling wind and rain.
> It is my heart that's late,
> it is my song that's flown.
> Outdoors all afternoon
> under a gunmetal sky
> staking my garden down,
> I kneeled to the crickets trilling
> underfoot as if about
> to burst from their crusty shells;
> and like a child again
> marveled to hear so clear
> and brave a music pour
> from such a small machine.

What makes the engine go?
Desire, desire, desire.
The longing for the dance
stirs in the buried life.
One season only,
and it's done.
So let the battered old willow
thrash against the windowpanes
and the house timbers creak.
Darling, do you remember
the man you married. Touch me,
remind me who I am.

The poem allows a number of correspondences to surface slowly—the storm outside, the memory of younger days when Kunitz was "wild with love" and incarnated that love in song, and the crickets, which that very afternoon trilled with such an outpouring of song, they seemed "as if about / to burst from their crusty shells." Listening to those crickets made Kunitz a "child again" and brought him to the child-like question the poem turns on: What makes the crickets sing as they do? The answer transcends time—"Desire, desire, desire"—and, while Kunitz readjusts his earlier line, recognizing it is his heart that's late and not the summer, he simultaneously understands it is never too late for the heart or the song. Both reside in the "buried life" and can be stirred—by memory, by a storm, by crickets. Like Keats, Kunitz hears crickets sing and, like Keats, seeks a "language that would incarnate the poetry of his blood" (Kunitz's phrase from his essay, "The Modernity of Keats"). Their singing reawakens the necessity for song; which is to say, the crickets awaken the "I am," those two words which the poem ends on and that declare the fullness of our being always waiting to be touched into life. As Stanley Kunitz did, again and again, over a lifetime of one hundred years.

Browning's Villains

A S AN UNDERGRADUATE IN a state college, I read an essay by
Howard Moss, a poet I admired and the poetry editor of the *New
Yorker* at that time. Though his advice was of the usual "learn the tradition" school, what Moss said about writing poems struck the insecure
hyperconscious-of-my-poorly-educated-self hard—he said, unless a poet
knew the poems of the past, that poet was bound to repeat what another
poet had already done better. Solid, but obvious advice that, nevertheless, I took deeply to heart.

And so I went off to graduate school in English in 1972, closeting,
like many of my fellow graduate students, my desire to be a writer inside
the more mainline pursuit of a doctoral degree. In an early Victorian literature class, I first read Robert Browning. I was writing persona poems,
trying to find my own voice by assuming the guise of others. Struck by
the energy of Browning's dramatic monologues, I began to think about
the way he appropriated first-person narration and about the way his
poems worked dramatically, through their plots.

His "villains," in poems such as "Porphyria's Lover," "The Bishop
Orders His Tomb at Saint Praxed's Church," and the more famous, pos-
sessively titled, "My Last Duchess," all employed untrustworthy first-
person speakers that were allowed to convict themselves. And, while
Browning was clearly concerned with the immorality of villainy, his aim
was modern in so far as these were poems of the "act of the mind," as
Wallace Stevens would later define modern poetry. They were not about
ideas of pride and envy, or possessiveness and the love of material things,
but about the reader's experience of the villainy at the heart of them. Or
to put it another way, the reader's experience of the speaking voice, a
voice that created, as it went on talking, a kind of internal, if perverted,
order within the fictional entity of the poem.

In fact, Browning's contemporaries accused him of perversity; reading him, they found their sympathies aroused for characters that were, in large part, reprehensible. Of course, Browning never argued in these poems for the villainous ideas presented in the poems. He simply let the passion and will and intellectual fervor of his first-person speakers work their seductive charms. In "The Bishop Orders His Tomb at Saint Praxed's Church," the dying Renaissance bishop looks to get assurances from his sons that his tomb will outdo the tomb of Old Gandolf, his predecessor at Saint Praxed, who, in the bishop's mind has already "cozened" him out of the best spot in the church for his resting place. He wants his tomb to use

> Some lump, ah God, of *lapis lazuli,*
> Big as a Jew's head cut off at the nape,
> Blue as a vein o'er the Madonna's breast

for a globe that will be positioned between his knees on his effigy, a globe that will even outshine "God the Father's globe" in the Trinity sculpture, carved from the largest known block of lapis lazuli, at the baroque Jesuit church, Il Gesu, in Rome. The vulgar, bigoted slur, the eroticized breast of the Madonna, and the prideful one-upmanship of an even more magnificent globe of God's terrestrial creation, all arrive with such unapologetic energy we're almost thrilled to envision their ultimate purpose: to make Gandolf "see and burst." Browning allows us to convict ourselves.

When the bishop realizes his sons may not be buying into his "orders" for a "peach-blossom marble" slab and that terrestrial ball of lapis lazuli, he reminds them of the "villas, all" he has bequeathed them:

> Ah, ye hope
> To revel down my villas while I gasp
> Bricked o'er with beggar's moldy travertine.

And he plays the "woe-is-me" card of guilt: "Swift as a weaver's shuttle fleet our years: / Man goeth to the grave, and where is he?" He is, to answer the question in the bishop's own words, in need of a jasper slab and a bas-relief in bronze that mixes Pans and Nymphs and "the Savior at his sermon on the mount." The zest for living of the dying man, the no-holds-barred desire to get what he wants, and to do whatever it takes to realize those wants makes up Browning's plot. It's almost as hard for the reader to escape the bishop's designs as it is for his children.

But just about the time the bishop senses his children tiring of his material predilections and nearly pathological need to have a more opulent tomb than his clerical rival's, Browning's speaker divulges his darkest, underlying fears; the bishop fears, as many do, the tomb itself: "Clammy squares [of gritstone] which sweat / as if the corpse they keep were oozing through." The loved body lost, the dissolution of the very flesh through which the world's sensual pleasures are tasted: these fears are, perhaps, what keep the reader off-balance to the end, of two minds about our bishop.

If the reader sees the bishop's villainy and then suspends judgment, realizing as we do the bishop's very human needs in ourselves, the lover in "Porphyria's Lover" remains outside our sympathies. And yet once again Browning uses the dualities of his first-person speaker to complicate the reader's response. The speaker is mad. He strangles Porphyria with her own hair in order to preserve the moment when she surrenders her love to him. Browning's poem is driven by characterization and plot. Once the character and needs of Porphyria's lover are established, the poem makes the speaker's motives appear quite rational. He is a criminal because he loves and because he, in his own mad mind, has run through the "facts" more than once, and now simply completes the act which Porphyria, who has come through wind and rain and "made her smooth white shoulder bare . . . and, stooping, made my cheek lie there" is still too full of pride to do: "give herself to [him] forever." Once the plot is set in motion it cannot help but lead to this climactic moment:

> Be sure I looked up at her eyes
> > Happy and proud; at last I knew
> Porphyria worshipped me: surprise
> > Made my heart swell, and still it grew
> > While I debated what to do.
> That moment she was mine, mine, fair,
> > Perfectly pure and good: I found
> A thing to do, and all her hair
> > In one long yellow string I wound
> > Three times her little throat around,
> And strangled her. No pain felt she;
> > I am quite sure she felt no pain.

Of course Browning's lover is the classic untrustworthy narrator. We experience the entire evening through his perceptions. But Browning's speaker isn't psychologically deranged by some deep subconscious forces: he is full of refinement and kindness (mad as those qualities may be) and, after strangling Porphyria, lays her head on his shoulder, reciprocating her earlier act, and sees in her smile and eyes that all she feared and scorned—"to give herself to me forever"—has now completely "fled." He even wonders why, though they have stayed this way all night long, God has not "said a word" to bless this mad union.

Human will plays a leading role in "My Last Duchess" as well. And, once again, elements of fiction are here: a first person narrator/speaker, who tells the truth, though the truth here is entirely consistent with the character of the speaker; a rather intact fictional world conditioned by the historical time (Renaissance) the speaker inhabits and his own psychological habits of mind; and a plot that enjoys a kind of validity inside the poem but is morally problematic outside the poem's fictional world.

The engine of the poem is the Duke of Ferrara's untroubled belief in his own aristocratic values. The poem's outrageous plot: the cruel Italian duke out of unreasonable jealousy has had his last wife, the duchess of the title, murdered and is now contracting a second marriage for the dowry with the envoy of a prospective duchess. Now add this irony: the duke tells the story of "his" last duchess while showing off to the envoy the artistic merits of the last duchess's portrait, a painting so good it makes her look "as if she were alive." Following the duke and envoy down the stairway where the portrait hangs, the poem concludes at the bottom of the staircase with the duke bargaining for the dowry and showing yet another of his art "objects"—Neptune "taming a seahorse"—that displays defiantly both his taming and ultimately stilling (as the seahorse cast in bronze "for me" is stilled) of what belonged to him: his last duchess.

The duke's villainy, as all readers of this poem know, divides our moral judgment (he is reprehensible and proud of it) and our sympathies (we find his villainy the least interesting aspect of the poem) as we watch the duke command the situation with poise, arrogance, and sheer force of will. Like Milton's Satan, the Duke's thinking can make an atrocious act good and the good duchess bland and undiscriminating: she has a heart, in the duke's words, "too soon made glad, / Too easily impressed." Once we're inside the Duke's aristocratic spell, it is impossible to extricate ourselves; his hellishness becomes a heaven, and the duchess is summarily dismissed with this remark to the envoy:

> Sir, 'twas all one! My favor at her breast,
> The dropping of the daylight in the West,
> The bough of cherries some officious fool
> Broke in the orchard for her, the white mule
> She rode around the terrace—all and each
> Would draw from her alike the approving speech,
> Or blush, at least. She thanked men—good! but thanked
> Somehow—I know not how—as if she ranked
> My gift of a nine-hundred-years-old name

With anybody's gift.

The sheer verve of these lines, which convict our speaker, also suspend our judgment; we go along with the duke as he explains how he could have tried to discipline the duchess in the ways of her new station but, of course, that would have involved "stooping" and, as he announces with great bravado, "I choose never to stoop." What's a duke with a nine-hundred-year-old name to do?—why, give "commands" and stop altogether those silly, indiscriminate smiles. And there he is, confessing to having his last wife murdered to the envoy who he then asks to join him (allowing the envoy into his aristocratic orbit) and as they go off to "meet the company below."

The duke's sense of himself and his position, the outrageous staircase monologue that justifies his last duchess's murder with "what else could I do" and the contracting for his next duchess, who, presumably, will simply become another art possession, leaves the reader more giddy than troubled. Of course, Browning makes perfect use of the paradox at the heart of so many of his dramatic monologues—a first person speaker who, while reprehensible (and perhaps the more reprehensible the better) is perfectly at home in his own wickedness. Browning's characterization drives the action, and, within the world of the poem, the duke's actions seem almost natural. If we stop and ask what is the duke's motive—surely telling the story of the last duchess's demise and talking about the dowry can do him no good—we can only conclude that: the duke cannot help himself; or his speech forces the envoy into participating in the values of the duke's own world; or the duke cannot help himself because he assumes that the values he holds are incontrovertibly the only values that are right. The answer is probably all of the above.

Browning's villains—the first capable of guile and aesthetic appreciation; the second, a master of argument and rational thought (even when mad); and the third, an aristocrat possessing a straightforward, unquestioning belief in himself and his birthright—all keep the reader off-balance. If the reader sees the villainy in each of these characters, that judgment is by far the least interesting aspect of the poem. What is interesting: the pleasures of Browning's language, and how, once we indulge in those pleasures of voice, of characterization and character-driven plots, we cannot stand apart from the fictional world of the poem. We simply go along for the ride, never pausing to think too hard about the villains. Caught up in their worlds, we care only about what those villains will say or do next. And, when the poems finally reach their close and their imaginative hold relents, we come, at last, to see ourselves and how we are and are not like the bishop, or even Porphyria's lover, or that egregiously egotistic duke.

David Ferry

Ways of Asking

IN HIS POEM, "ADAM'S CURSE," the Irish poet William Butler Yeats voices the age-old complaint of writers, saying that despite how long it takes and how much effort goes into writing a good line of poetry, let alone a good poem, the public views the poet or writer as an "idler." In my house, the accusatory question went something like this: why are you lying around on the couch; or why are you just sitting there, staring off into the woods? My answer: I'm writing. I could have added, way too defensively, that my lying around was hard work. *Hard work?*—absolutely, since each poem requires something new, presents a new task, asks for a new voice, asks, it seems, to be plucked out of thin air and somehow embodied in words that are still hovering, waiting to be named. And I haven't yet named the hardest work of all: attentiveness to one's own emotions, emotions that are, more often than not, contradictory and painful.

Writing, in other words, requires time, and a poem or story or art in general needs time to percolate emotionally so that it can become more than personal expression. If, as another Yeats poem, "Meditations in Time of Civil War," puts it—"only an aching heart / conceives a changeless work of art"—then we write because our hearts ache. But heartache alone does not make a "work of art." Our heartache needs "form" as Yeats well knew. It needs to be "conceived": imagined, made into a plan, and conceived like a child.

The lines I quoted from the poem concern a five-hundred-year-old Japanese sword Yeats kept on his desk to remind himself of the generations of traditional sword-making techniques that went into the making of a "changeless work of art." Or to put that sentiment in a less lofty way, we need to consider the hard work of finding a form that will allow others to participate in the heartache of being human rather than feel sorry for our personal heartache.

When I say form, I don't necessarily mean to imply only the usual, time-tested forms of elegy or ode, sonnet or villanelle. Or a standard meter and rhyme. And, while I do mean something like Alexander Pope's notion that poems select and place the "best possible words in the best possible order," that's not all I mean. In the best poems, the form allows the personal to become impersonal, or to say that in a better way, what is personal in the poem moves beyond mere personality.

But let's start with heartache. Most of us who write, write first out of some form of heartache. That heartache can be routine and trivial (though never trivial to the person who is suffering it) or enormous and life-shattering: from a fight with a friend at school to the incomprehensibleness of a child dying of cancer. Heartache can span the break-up of a three-week relationship and the death of someone we loved for thirty years; it can span the insult heaped on us in the school lunchroom and our existential angst, false or true, over the daily injustices occurring every minute in every place around the world. Which is to say heartache begins in the contradictions of living: we feel the unbridgeable distances between the way we think things should be and the way things are. Those unbridgeable distances may occur in the world we live in where bad things do indeed happen to good people and, where almost daily, we feel the continuous human need for love and the frequent inability to give it; or we might first feel that unbridgeable distance in ourselves: between who we might be or even have strived to become and the person we actually are.

The Nobel-prize winning poet, Czeslaw Milosz, put it this way: we live a kind of double life because of our "common human circumstances as beings in between the dust that we are and the divinity to which we would aspire." And long before Milosz, Plato saw our predicament quite similarly: he said that the situation of the human being is always "en route," never quite arriving, always living "in between" what is comprehensible and what remains a mystery.

The question I asked when I was much younger is one I'm still asking over forty-five years later: Why, if there is so much injustice in the world, so much unaccountable suffering, so many wars and seemingly endless bigotry, so much fear in living in a world that is both so vast and so indifferent to our individual suffering, do we still take such joy in being alive? In many ways, everything I have ever written has been in response to that question. In one of his comedy routines, the comedian

Louis C. K. jokes about what you get with the basic life. As he puts it, even with the boiler plate deal, with basic cable life, you get to live on earth. And that is an amazing gift. Life, and not even a particularly lucky life, is an amazing gift: as Louis C. K. puts it, "you get to be on earth and look at shit."

"Looking at shit" is where most of our questions come from. That's not a joke. I genuinely feel that I should "apologize," as Szymborska has said, "to time for all the world I overlook each second." So asking begins with looking. But looking isn't as easy as it sounds. Remember the religious concept of the *via negativa,* or the practice of "cleaning house," of negating all human constructed images of God in order to allow in the immanent energies of God. I think looking at shit requires the same kind of house cleaning. Consider this statement from Thoreau: "I begin to see an object when I cease to understand it." When I first read that statement I was annoyed. I took it as some ill-founded anti-intellectual bias from a guy who'd said to Emerson he could eat a woodchuck raw. But I came to realize how Thoreau was referring to the illusory power that knowledge can confer. Often, when we think we understand something, our thinking ends. We stop seeing things because we think we know them. Just consider how the buildings and trees on your routes around town have disappeared as you named them Town Hall, Bank of America, Elm and Maple, and then forgot about them.

So far I have made three points: first, that form allows what is personal in the poem to move beyond mere personality; second, that poems arise out of our *in-betweeness* and those three little words "I don't know"; and third, that our questions about life and whatever partial answers we arrive at comes from "looking at shit" as if for the first time.

I want to look now at a poem by David Ferry that embodies these three points. The poem is called "Lake Water" and it was first published in *The New Yorker* in 2008. It became part of Ferry's latest book of poems, *Bewilderment,* which won the National Book Award for Poetry in 2012 when Ferry was 88. David is better known as a translator—of *Gilgamesh,* of Horace's *Odes* and *Epistles* and Virgil's *Eclogues* and *Georgics*—and, most recently—of the *Aeneid.*

But he is a poet first of all, and he is one of our best. David is 95 now. I say David because he is a friend. His wife, Anne, whose death "Lake Water" is about, was my graduate school teacher. Because of this friendship, I know many of the personal aspects of this poem. I want to consider today how Ferry has found a form that transfigures what was messy and painful in the most profoundly personal ways into a poem that is profoundly beautiful without ever trying to escape that pain. It is a poem that lives in the "in-between" of what can and cannot be said and known. And, finally, it is a poem that looks at a lake that Ferry knew all of his adult life—Lake Waban on the campus of Wellesley College where he taught for forty or so years.

In his collection of poems, *Of No Country I Know*, Ferry dedicates the book "To Anne" and then adds this translation of Scottish poetry known as the Bannatyne Manuscript:

> My married heart shall never turn from her
>> Unto another so long as my five wits
> Shall last, whose whole consent is given to her
>> Until death's rage shall cleave me to the root.
> So shall I love her ever, in spite of what-
>> Soever circumstances can do to us.
> God grant I go the grave before she does.

Of course, Anne went to the grave before him. They were married for nearly fifty years. Anne Ferry wrote seven books of criticism, all on poetry, and she was perhaps the best close reader of poetry I ever knew. And she was David's best reader, tuned as she was to the line and the syntactical strategies of the sentence. Anne was fiercely intelligent and could always find the exact words to coax a Herbert poem or a Shakespeare sonnet into that network of connections where poems become an experience rather than an intellectual exercise. And so the last years of her life were particularly painful: she suffered from aphasia, a condition that robs a person of the ability to communicate. It affected her ability to speak, write, and understand the very language she loved.

That theft, and the love for a wife who was now, to use David's word, "unreadable," is part of the title of David's book, *Bewilderment*, and the way that word holds inside it both the wild and the archaic *wilder* through which one wanders in the confusions of bewilderment. And it's the story behind "Lake Water."

The poem opens with a declarative sentence, but its casual observation becomes the rhetorical strategy of the poem: "It is a summer afternoon in October." What will be seen in the hesitating, self-adjusting sentences that follow—sentences which merely look at the lake and the weather, but are driven by Szymborska's "I don't know"—why the day is like this or why it would arouse in me the feelings that there is more going on here than just the unusually hot weather. Just as the weather is wrong for the time of year, so too does something seem out-of-sorts; there's something about this pastoral harmony that is slightly ajar, and, as the poem will make clear, the "truth" that is "being told" will not be easily found.

Before I launch into a reading of the poem, I want to pause a moment and define the way I'm using the word *form*. In the broadest sense, the simplest requirement of form is the expectation that each element of a poem is part of the shaped experience of its whole. We expect a word's placement, the choice of this or that image, the sound of the poem and the syntactical structure of its sentences and use of the line, and even its punctuation, to be purposeful, not accidental, and always contributing at least a part of the answer to these basic rhetorical questions: Why am I being told these things? Who is speaking and to whom and to what end is this speaker speaking?

Every poem, that is, has a rhetorical structure that helps to move the poem from the realm of personal experience into the realm of universal experience. These simple questions should force the writer to ask much harder questions: what do I find interesting about this event? Why did it press on me with its peculiar weight and significance? What was particular and specific to this event? Poems keep circling an experience, looking to make sense of it, both in terms of the writer's and reader's experience.

That said, let's look more closely at Ferry's poem, "Lake Water." The title of the poem tells us nothing and then, of course, everything. I say nothing because, at first the title seems to be simply what the poem is about: a man looking at a lake, particularly the breezes that scallop and riffle the water, and the qualities of the October day and how they affect the plane of water. By the end of the poem, we realize that the lake water has become both a metaphor for a page of writing and for the dying face of a loved one. And we learn, finally, that what lies behind all the hesitations and qualifications and "as ifs" of the speaker, behind those basically iambic lines peppered with anapests, and behind this near-obsessive look at the lake water, is the speaker's grief, grief over—let's say it directly now—a long-loved wife whose death was as natural and "unreadable" as the lake water and the strange summer-like October day.

True enough. But my interest is in how Ferry's sentences and their syntactical strategies enlarge the poem. While the grief in this poem is personal and deeply moving, the poem is not simply about David's grief over Anne's aphasia and death. It is a poem, of course, that becomes a meditation on language and what language can and cannot do. And it is a poem that captures what I said earlier about the opaque nature of reality: that the imagination here that presses up against that opacity senses the way the water, and life in general, is more meaningful than we can say, and yet our saying, our "figures of speech" are what we have to register that feeling of being in the presence of some "origination," something momentous that goes on revealing and concealing itself.

Ferry's first stanza is composed of five sentences. There are two simple declarative sentences: "It is a summer afternoon in October" and "Seen twice it seemed a truth was being told." We might say the other three, longer, more clausal sentences complicate what the shorter sentences declare:

> It is a summer afternoon in October.
> I am sitting on a wooden bench, looking out
> At the lake through a tall screen of evergreens,
> Or rather, looking out across the plane of the lake,
> Seeing the light shaking upon the water
> As if it were a shimmering of heat.
> Yesterday, when I sat here it was the same,
> The same displaced out-of-season effect.
> Seen twice it seemed a truth was being told.
> Some of the trees I can see across the lake
> Have begun to change, but it is as if the air
> Had entirely given itself over to summer
> With the intention of denying its own proper nature.

Note how the second sentence complicates the "looking out" (which is already complicated in the play of the words—both a seeing across the lake and a "looking out" for what could emerge from this strange day. But Ferry's syntax is crucial: he is looking out, both through a "screen of evergreens" and looking out "across the plane of lake" (literally because he is sitting down, and the surface is all he can see).

But his phrase "Or rather" complicates the act of looking out. So does the next hesitation: "as if it were a shimmering of heat." One thing ("light shaking on the water") looks like another ("a shimmering of heat"). And that duality is complicated further by the pronoun in the following sentence: "Yesterday when I sat here it was the same," where "it" can refer to the plane of the lake, the light looking like heat, and the possibility that yesterday felt like summer in October.

If there is a truth being told as the second declarative sentence tells us, it is far from a simple truth. The truth here is something like the "air" which, being October air, should be getting colder, but is "denying its proper nature" by giving itself over to summer warmth. All is "as if," the speaker's mind reaching out to one analogy after another, as we all do, to make sense of things, to bring the unfamiliar back into the realm of the familiar. Even Ferry's line disorients in the same way, often appearing to be iambic pentameter, but wavering between five and six stresses and filled with anapests that skip along, slipping out of the pentameter metronome.

Stanzas two, three, and four work similarly, introducing a "breeze" that changes and changes the already changing light and makes it seem, in its steady pushing of waves against the shore, as if the lake was tidal. As before, these small disturbances of the familiar, suggest some darker forces are at play. And, as in the earlier stanzas, Ferry's lines and sentences carry his meaning: there is a "steady breeze" blowing, though where that breeze is coming from—simply the other side of the lake or from a place "beyond" the other side—is unclear. The breeze seems both this- and other-worldly. Moreover, it is hard to discriminate between the effects of the light and the effects of the breeze on the light. The breeze creates light and shadow and "alterations" in the light of the sun on the water. And, just for the fun of it, the poem tosses in the shadow of a cloud and its effects.

But all this obsessive looking at and recording of the light and water and breezes would be just that—obsessive and tiresome—if they were not connected to something larger in the rhetorical strategy of the poem. They are. Both the hesitating syntax and the brooding and repetitious scouring of the minute changes in what is happening contribute to the creation of the speaker and the answer, at least in part, to why this particular speaker is speaking.

While the speaker is, of course, David Ferry, it is also a fictional David Ferry, a character named David Ferry who can, in the midst of a carefully constructed sentence, blurt out "there's something infantile / About it, a baby at the breast." Think of how perfect that dash is—in the midst of talking about the "mild sound" of the "tapping waves"; in the midst of rocking us in that cradle of sounds, "The mild sound of the little tapping waves / The breeze has caused," Ferry suddenly breaks off his sentence to tell us a little about what he must be feeling. And his feelings, at least to his mind, are infantile, "a baby at the breast."

The analogy, like all analogies in poems, tells us more about the speaker than about what is being compared. Our speaker is speaking because he wants succor rather than confusion. His emotions have been "concentrated," as he puts it, by the breezy light and the waves lapping at the shoreline and now he's become, in the dramatic arc of the poem, aware of them. He's aware that the sounds are "decidedly sexual," and that he has regressed in his grief to something like a nursing child. Of course, what we know from the end of the poem is that our speaker,

David Ferry, has lost the loved body of his wife in death. He wants an "infantile obliviousness," free of the painful loss he carries with him wherever he goes. He wants, as Job wanted after his afflictions, to be back in the womb, to be back with the water at the point of origination.

If the reader has wondered where all these observations about the day's weather were headed, stanza five provides the answers. It is the longest stanza in the poem and the stanza is one long sentence. And its self-conscious figure of the lake water as a page of writing has been carefully prepared for dramatically by the burgeoning self-consciousness in the poem of its speaker. Yes, the lake water is like a page on which this very poem or every poem for that matter is being written:

> The plane of the water is like a page on which
> Phrases and even sentences are written,
> But because of the breeze, and the turning of the year,
> And the sense that this lake water, as it is being
> Experienced on a particular day, comes from
> Some source somewhere, beneath, within, itself,
> Or from somewhere else, nearby, a spring, a brook,
> Its pure origination somewhere else,
> It is like an idea for a poem not yet written
> And maybe never to be completed, because
> The surface of the page is like lake water,
> That takes back what is written on its surface,
> And all my language about the lake and its
> Emotions or its sweet obliviousness,
> Or even its being like an origination,
> Is all erased with the changing of the breeze
> Or because of the heedless passing of a cloud.

Suddenly we realize why the lake has been the focus of the speaker's seemingly endless and obsessive considerations. Entering directly into the poem with "all my language," Ferry makes clear that all this considering and re-considering has been an attempt to make sense of the welter of emotions that concentrate themselves as if some epiphany or understanding were arriving and then dissolved.

But it's the form of this stanza's sentence which embodies that idea for us. Its phrasings build and build—the water is like a page on which phrases, then sentences, are written, and as these sentences are being written they are like an idea for a poem and then a poem that may never be completed. And all these words, phrases, sentences, possible poems are arising out of "some source somewhere, beneath, within, itself, or from somewhere else." Ferry's syntax bodies forth both the mystery of poems' origins, how they are not there on the page and then there, and it captures how we often feel that life (i.e., the lake water) is more meaningful than we can know and yet, while what we are experiencing may exceed our language's reach, it is still a kind of knowing, a sense that we are in the presence of something larger that is revealing itself even as it is ultimately concealed once again.

Of course Ferry realizes our language is, as Keats put it in his epitaph, "writ on water," "erased with the changing of the breeze / Or because of the heedless passing of a cloud." And, even more painfully, Ferry acknowledges that what we can know about death and even the face of someone we have loved for fifty years, is "unreadable." The novelist Philip Roth has said that the one task of the writer is "not to simplify . . . not to erase the contradiction, not to deny the contradiction, but to see where, within the contradiction, lies the tormented human being."

David Ferry's poem begins with and remains loyal to Szymborska's three little words, "I don't know." Like Roth, he remains in that "in-between," allowing us to see what he can know and not know, what can ease his grief and what cannot. And he reminds us that what we have is our "figures of speech," which try to circle and shape a reality that is intelligible, if not knowable. What we have is the forms we make to ease our aching hearts, and the hearts of others who, as fellow human beings, cannot help but ache.

Acknowledgments

Grateful acknowledgment is made to the following journals, in which many of these essays were first published, sometimes in a slightly different version and with a slightly different title:

The Alabama Review: "The Longest Day"

Image: "Finding the 'World's Fullness'"; "The Revolt Against Narcissus"; "Cloud Shapes and Oak Trees"; "Acts of Attention: Reflections on Poetry and Spirituality"; "Love Calls Us to One World at a Time"; "The Art of Devotion: On Poetry and Prayer"; "On Mystery"

Lutheran Forum: "Metaphors to Live In"; "A Certain Young Man"

McMaster Journal of Theology and Ministry: "'To Discover an Order as of a Season': Some Thoughts on Nature Poetry"

New Ohio Review: "Browning's Villains"

Poetry Daily: "George Herbert's *Jordan 2*"

Semeia: "Something More"

Worcester Review: "The Otherworldliness of Elizabeth Bishop"

"Touch Me" from *Passing Through* by Stanley Kunitz. Reprinted by permission of W. W. Norton & Company.

"Meditations at Lagunitas" from *Praise* by Robert Haas. Reprinted by permission of HarperCollins Publishers.

This book was set in Sabon, designed by the German typographer and book designer, Jan Tschichold, and released in 1967. Tschichold was inspired to design Sabon after encountering a sixteenth-century specimen sheet produced by the legendary printer and typographer, Claude Garamond (1480–1561). The typeface is named after one of Garamond's students and colleagues, Jacques Sabon (1535–ca. 1580–90).

This book was designed by Ian Creeger, Jim Tedrick, and Gregory Wolfe. It was published in hardcover, paperback, and electronic formats by Slant Books, Seattle, WA.

The cover was designed by Jim Tedrick and Gregory Wolfe.

The cover image is *Jacob and the Angel (Study)*, ca. 1876, by Léon Joseph Florentin Bonnat, in the collection of *Musée Bonnat-Helleu*, Bayonne, France.

www.ingramcontent.com/pod-product-compliance
Lightning Source LLC
Chambersburg PA
CBHW022011050726
47499CB00007BA/2210